My eLab | Efficient teaching, effective learning

My eLab is the interactive environment that gives you access to self-graded exercises related to your coursebook. Thanks to your personal dashboard, you can easily view your progress, as well as any upcoming assignments. Be sure to register for **My eLab** to ensure your success!

email rep
CC: Sabina

D0165236

TO REGISTER

❶ Go to **http://mybookshelf.pearsonerpi.com**

❷ Click on "**NOT REGISTERED YET?**" and follow the instructions. When asked for your access code, please type the code provided underneath the blue sticker.

❸ To access **My eLab** at any time, go to http://mybookshelf.pearsonerpi.com. **Bookmark this page for quicker access.**

Access to My eLab is valid for 6 months from the date of registration.

STUDENT ACCESS CODE

LA06ST-RADII-POESY-HUMAN-CHAIR-CHASE

WARNING! This book CANNOT BE RETURNED if the access code has been uncovered.

Note: Once you have registered, you will need to join your online class. Ask your teacher to provide you with the class ID.

TEACHER Access Code

To obtain an access code for My eLab, please contact your Pearson ELT consultant.

1 800 263-3678
assistance@pearsonerpi.com

🐦 @HelpPearsonERPI

W135229 (A36731)

leapadvanced

LISTENING AND SPEAKING

Learning English for Academic Purposes

PEARSON

Montréal

Managing Editor
Patricia Hynes

Project Editor
Linda Barton

Copy Editor
Stacey Berman

Proofreader
Mairi MacKinnon

Coordinator, Rights and Permissions
Pierre Richard Bernier

Art Director
Hélène Cousineau

Graphic Design Coordinator
Lyse LeBlanc

Book and Cover Design
Frédérique Bouvier

Book Layout
Interscript

The publisher thanks the following people for their helpful comments and suggestions:

Susan A. Curtis, University of British Columbia

Joanna Daley, Kwantlen Polytechnic University

Kristibeth Kelly Delgado, Fanshaw College

Michelle Duhaney, Seneca College

Joan Dundas, Brock University

Linda Feuer, University of Manitoba

Carleen Gruntman, Université Laval

Brianna Hilman, University of Calgary

Marcia Kim, University of Calgary

Izabella Kojic-Sabo, University of Windsor

Jennifer Layte, University of Manitoba

Catherine Lemay, Université Laval

Brooke Mills, Kwantlen Polytechnic University

Tania Pattison, Trent University

Karen Rauser, University of British Columbia, Okanagan Campus

Cyndy Reimer, Douglas College

Tanya Seredynska, HEC Montréal

© ÉDITIONS DU RENOUVEAU PÉDAGOGIQUE INC. (ERPI), 2013
ERPI publishes and distributes PEARSON ELT products in Canada.

5757 Cypihot Street
Saint-Laurent, Québec H4S 1R3
CANADA
Telephone: 1 800 263-3678
Fax: 1 866 334-0448
infoesl@pearsonerpi.com
http://pearsonelt.ca

Registration of copyright – Bibliothèque et Archives nationales du Québec, 2013
Registration of copyright – Library and Archives Canada, 2013

Printed in Canada   34567890   SO   17 16 15 14
ISBN 978-2-7613-5229-1   135229 ABCD   OF10

Dedication

To all teachers who (to paraphrase Henry B. Adams) affect eternity, never knowing where their influence stops. And, for eternal light and laughter, thanks to my wife, Ann, and sons, Nathan and Spencer.

Audio and Video Text Credits

Chapter 1, p. 6 "How to Be Innovative in Your Business" © 2012 Small Business Big Marketing. p. 12 "The Economics of Mass Collaboration" © 2010 Harvard Business School Publishing. All rights reserved. p. 16 "The DNA of the World's Most Innovative Companies" reproduced courtesy of INSEAD Knowledge (http://knowledge.insead.edu) © INSEAD 2011.

Chapter 2, p. 26 "The Seven Deadly Sins of Business Ethics" © 2011 The Ethical Society of St. Louis. p. 32 "Room to Read's John Wood: Bringing the Power of Education to Children around the World" reproduced with permission from Knowledge@Wharton © 2008 Knowledge@Wharton. All rights reserved. p. 37 "Poverty Is a Threat to Peace" © Nobel Media AB (2006).

Chapter 3, p. 49 "What Is Cybernetics?" and "Implants to Improve Impaired Vision" © 2012 The Naked Scientists. p. 53 "Cynthia Breazeal–Personal Robots" reproduced with permission of EPFL, Switzerland. p. 59 "Full Interview: Ayesha Khanna on Smart Cities and the Hybrid Age" © Canadian Broadcasting Corporation.

Chapter 4, p. 69 "Sustainable Urban Development to 2050" © 2010 University of Oxford, reproduced with permission of the speaker. pp. 74, 78 "Sustainability: The Next Management Frontier" © 2011 MIT, reproduced with permission of the speakers.

Chapter 5, p. 89 "Julie Posetti on Making Journalism Social: Twitter's Transformative Effect" reproduced with permission of the Wheeler Centre. p. 94 "Breaking News: The Changing Relationship between Blogs and Mainstream Media" © Oxford Internet Institute, University of Oxford. p. 100 "Emily Bell on the Future of Online Journalism" © Canadian Broadcasting Corporation.

Chapter 6, p. 109 "The Creative Brain" adapted from *The Brain and Emotional Intelligence: New Insights* by Daniel Goleman © Daniel Goleman 2011. p. 113 "Gerard Darby: Science and Creativity" BBC © 2013. p. 117 "Creative Confidence: Cultivating the Mindset of Today's Innovators" reproduced courtesy of IDEO.

Chapter 7, p. 131 "Henrietta Lacks" © Canadian Broadcasting Corporation. p. 135 "In the Dissection Room" and "Donated to Science" © 2011 The Naked Scientists. p. 142 "Investigating the Ills of Long-Dead Celebrities" reproduced with permission from AAAS.

Chapter 8, p. 150 "Jane Goodall on Environmental Ethics" © Canadian Broadcasting Corporation. pp. 154, 161 "David Suzuki's Legacy" reproduced with permission of the David Suzuki Foundation.

INTRODUCTION

The *LEAP: Listening and Speaking* series focuses on critical thinking and language skills necessary for success in college and university. *LEAP Advanced: Listening and Speaking* maintains the series' cross-curricular approach, giving students opportunities to explore complex content from a range of subject areas, delivered by international experts. These experts span the world of English accents, including those of non-native speakers, to give advanced students varied and authentic listening experiences.

Students using *LEAP Advanced: Listening and Speaking* will meet with challenging ideas and engage in critical thinking and discussions on open-ended questions. In each chapter, students listen to material representing different formats and perspectives as they work toward individual speaking opportunities and group interactions in a variety of formal and informal contexts, from an elevator pitch to a seminar discussion to a town hall meeting. Through various types of structured activities, students build their vocabulary and comprehension of concepts in key academic disciplines. Each chapter features Focus on Speaking, Focus on Listening and Academic Survival Skill sections that students put into practice in Warm-Up Assignments and in the more substantial Final Assignments. To help students step back and think critically about paired chapter themes, Critical Connections offers opportunities to complete integrated tasks.

In an ever-changing world, students need critical-thinking and interaction skills. *LEAP Advanced: Listening and Speaking* explores the subtleties of language and communication, guiding students to interpret and express informed, compelling and persuasive messages.

ACKNOWLEDGEMENTS

A book such as this is built on countless consultations with teachers who give their time and insights to help develop print and online materials that will better address learners' needs. My deepest thanks to all those who shared questions and thoughts at conferences or who wrote reviews and suggestions, especially Susan Curtis and Jas Gill of the University of British Columbia.

Thanks also to my clever and ever-industrious editors, Patricia Hynes and Linda Barton, and to the entire Pearson Canada team. And, finally, thanks to Julia Williams, who wrote the first edition of *LEAP* and who writes the *Reading and Writing* books in this series.

HIGHLIGHTS

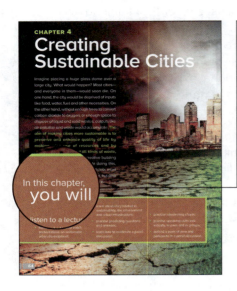

The **overview** outlines the chapter features and expectations.

The **Gearing Up** section features diagrams and images to spark critical thinking and discussion about the chapter topic.

Vocabulary Build sections develop comprehension of key vocabulary, including Academic Word List content, and reinforce acquisition through varied tasks.

Three **listening** excerpts offer different perspectives on the chapter theme, paired with critical-thinking activities to encourage reflection and prepare students for the speaking tasks.

Before You Listen activities elicit students' prior knowledge of a topic and stimulate interest.

While You Listen engages students in a variety of active listening strategies, including different approaches to note taking.

After You Listen asks students to critically reflect on and discuss personal or larger issues related to what they have heard or seen.

The **Warm-Up Assignment** gives students the opportunity to work on individual, pair or group presentations in preparation for the Final Assignment.

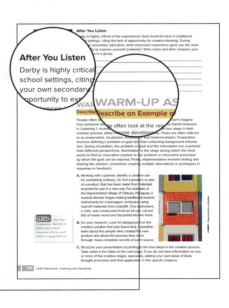

Focus on Listening

raises students' awareness of listening subskills so they can critically decode and interpret what they hear in the listening excerpts.

Focus on Speaking

builds students' confidence by exploring common speaking skills and presentation techniques.

Sidebars clarify and enliven learning.

Academic Survival Skills

help students understand and practise effective critical-thinking and presentation skills.

After every second chapter, a **Critical Connections** section encourages students to think critically about their learning, analyzing and synthesizing ideas in reflective discussion tasks.

References to the **Companion Website Plus** point students toward additional content, practice and support.

The Final Assignment

integrates everything a student has learned in the chapter and provides an opportunity to do research, structure content and apply speaking skills in a presentation or discussion.

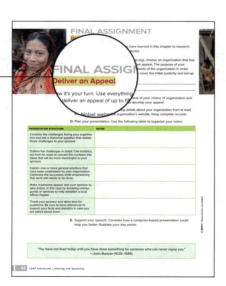

SCOPE AND SEQUENCE

CHAPTER	LISTENING	SPEAKING
CHAPTER 1 **PATHS TO INNOVATION** SUBJECT AREAS: business, marketing, technology	• Listening actively to three interviews • Understanding the purposes of repetition • Identifying main ideas to complete a flow chart	• Adding emphasis with intonation and stress • Speaking to a group to elicit support
CHAPTER 2 **THE BUSINESS OF HELPING OTHERS** SUBJECT AREAS: business, education, ethics	• Listening actively to two lectures and an interview • Identifying your expectations of a speech • Understanding facts and figures	• Using rhythm and structure effectively • Delivering a short persuasive speech
CHAPTER 3 **MACHINES IN YOUR FUTURE** SUBJECT AREAS: cybernetics, medicine, psychology	• Listening actively to three interviews • Relating definitions and explanations • Tying interview questions to answers	• Asking different kinds of questions to elicit specific responses • Framing a presentation with opening and closing statements
CHAPTER 4 **CREATING SUSTAINABLE CITIES** SUBJECT AREAS: environmental studies, technology, urban planning	• Listening actively to an interview, a lecture and a panel discussion • Predicting questions and answers • Identifying key facts to complete a flow chart	• Moderating a panel discussion • Defending a point of view
CHAPTER 5 **RISE OF THE CITIZEN JOURNALIST** SUBJECT AREAS: ccommunications, journalism, political science	• Listening actively to two lectures and an interview • Identifying repair, qualification and elaboration techniques • Listening in order to interrupt politely	• Explaining new ideas through comparisons • Asking questions for clarification
CHAPTER 6 **THE SCIENCE OF CREATIVITY** SUBJECT AREAS: design, education, neurology	• Listening actively to an audiobook excerpt and two lectures • Assessing technical details • Listening in order to challenge an argument	• Explaining abstract ideas through examples • Arguing for and against creative solutions
CHAPTER 7 **BODY OF RESEARCH** SUBJECT AREAS: medical ethics, medical research, pathology	• Listening actively to three interviews • Understanding the purposes of paraphrase • Listening for redundancy	• Conducting an informed interview • Role-playing to discuss speculative information
CHAPTER 8 **SAVING PLANET EARTH** SUBJECT AREAS: ecology, environmental ethics	• Listening actively to an interview, a lecture and audience questions after a lecture • Evaluating audience questions • Listening for forceful repetition	• Introducing a speaker • Signposting a presentation to engage listeners

ACADEMIC SURVIVAL SKILL	ASSIGNMENTS	CRITICAL THINKING
• Presenting a project proposal about an innovative idea	• Critiquing a product or service in a short presentation (5 min) • Proposing a product or service innovation in a group presentation (15 min)	• Challenging one's comfort zone • Structuring a critique • Predicting innovations in business
• Working with statistics to make numbers memorable	• Giving an elevator pitch to elicit support for a good cause (3 min) • Delivering an appeal to solicit sponsor support (15 min)	• Reflecting on metaphor in business contexts • Assessing the impact of social interventions • Evaluating ethical decisions
• Creating Likert-scale questions to measure attitudes	• Researching and explaining a technical subject related to medical technology (5 min) • Giving a presentation with a partner on physical or mental enhancements (10 min)	• Assessing attitudes toward cybernetics • Balancing ethical concerns in organ donations • Mapping areas for further research
• Interpreting charts to point out and clarify key features	• Discussing utopian and dystopian views of urban futures (10 min) • Participating in a panel discussion on potential sustainable initiatives (30 min)	• Ranking issues in order of importance • Examining initiatives to determine efficacy • Outlining potential urban legacies
• Organizing a news story using the inverted pyramid format	• Preparing a short podcast about a news event (5 min) • Taking part in an interview based on a news event (15 min)	• Evaluating the role of social media in communication • Evaluating short-term and long-term impacts of social media on journalism • Reflecting on the balance between privacy and service
• Identifying problems and evaluating arguments	• Describing an example of the creative process (10 min) • Taking part in a creative consultation to develop innovative solutions (15 min)	• Initiating creative problem solving • Relating a creative process to everyday objects and processes • Adopting different roles to critique an idea
• Practising the Harkness method of student-centred discussion	• Preparing a presentation to participate in a seminar on body donations (10 min) • Taking part in a seminar on the implications of donating one's body to science (60 min)	• Assessing the value of a medical contribution • Debating the ethics of sharing medical information • Analyzing key aspects of an idea
• Learning discussion techniques for examining problems	• Researching a speaker's background and introducing him or her to an audience (5 min) • Taking part in a town hall meeting on an environmental topic (60 min)	• Debating the relative worth of species • Evaluating greed versus need • Evaluating attitudes toward environmental issues

TABLE OF CONTENTS

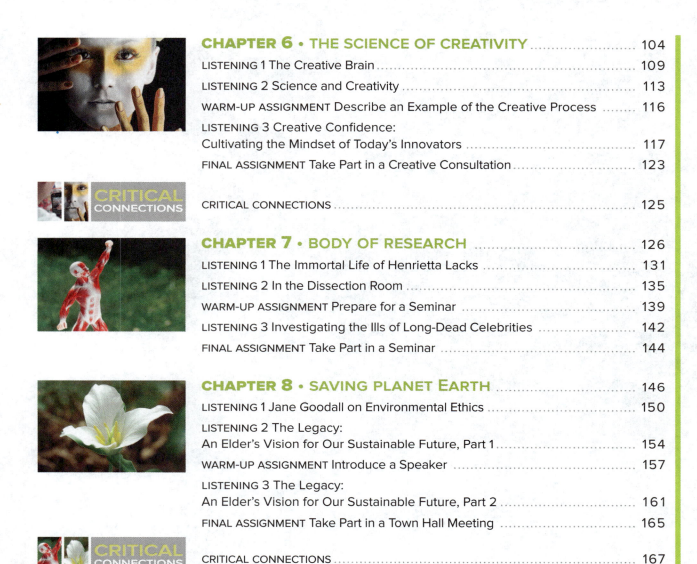

CHAPTER 1

Paths to Innovation

As consumers, we're fascinated by innovative products and services, from the latest phones to online news sites. Part of the attraction is seeing how products are incrementally improved to make our lives more efficient, attractive and exciting. Some of the most successful businesses are those that understand the value of these improvements and spend time and money on the research and development of new ideas. **But what makes an individual or a company innovative? Can the secrets of innovation be broken down into rules that can be understood, taught and applied to the next great innovation?**

In this chapter, you will

- listen to interviews about innovative individuals and businesses;

- learn vocabulary related to innovation and creativity;

- focus on listening for repetition;

- practise adding emphasis with intonation and stress;

- learn how to prepare a project proposal;

- practise speaking individually, in pairs and in groups;

- critique a product or service and prepare and deliver a group project proposal.

GEARING UP

A. Everyday objects often represent a long series of innovations. Look at the telephones above and number them to reflect their order of development, from the earliest (1) to the most recent (6).

B. Work with a partner and discuss the changes in the telephone over the years.

- What innovations do you see in each model?
- What new materials, technologies and needs might have led to each innovation?

C. Share your answers in a group.

A. Below are key words and phrases you will hear in Listening 1. Check the words you understand. Then, check the words you use.

	UNDERSTAND	USE		UNDERSTAND	USE
biases* (n.)	☐	☐	innovators* (n.)	☐	☐
break out of that rut (v.)	☐	☐	killer questions (n.)	☐	☐
comfort zone (n.)	☐	☐	out of your chair (adv.)	☐	☐
commitment* (n.)	☐	☐	peter out (v.)	☐	☐
configuration (n.)	☐	☐	positioning (v.)	☐	☐
conventions (n.)	☐	☐	reckon (v.)	☐	☐
disseminating (v.)	☐	☐	revenue* (n.)	☐	☐
diversity (n.)	☐	☐	right off the bat (adv.)	☐	☐
fallacy (n.)	☐	☐	scribe (n.)	☐	☐
implementer* (n.)	☐	☐	throw a curveball (v.)	☐	☐

*Appears on the Academic Word List

B. Write a definition for each of the words or phrases you do not understand, using a dictionary and continuing on a separate sheet of paper if necessary.

WORD/PHRASE	DEFINITION

C. In many words that begin with *com-* or *con-*, such as *commitment* and *configuration*, the meaning of the prefix is "with" or "together." Look at the following word stems and add *com-* or *con-* to complete the words. Look up definitions for the words you don't recognize.

_____ fluence	_____ pact	_____ press	_____ temporary	_____ vene
_____ join	_____ pel	_____ sequence	_____ tract	_____ verge

D. The expression *comfort zone* refers to feelings of competence and ease experienced in familiar situations. Write a paragraph outlining what you believe you could do to move out of your comfort zone and further develop your interests. For example, despite being in your comfort zone speaking another language, using that language to start a business in another culture might be outside your comfort zone. In your paragraph, use at least five words or phrases from task A.

_____

_____

_____

_____

_____

_____

_____

E. Work in a small group and read and discuss your paragraphs. Look for similarities and differences inside and outside group members' comfort zones.

FOCUS ON LISTENING

Listening for Repetition

You might have read about a presentation in advance or have clues about its content from the context. However, when you are actually listening to a presentation, it might be difficult to remember all the main ideas; you need clues as to what is important. Words and phrases that are repeated can help you identify main ideas, even if you miss the beginning of the talk. Sometimes repetition stresses key words. Other times, signalling words and phrases are repeated to point out main ideas.

A. Read the following excerpt from Listening 1 and consider how certain clues help the listener. Highlight the words and phrases that are repeated.

Defines "creativity," repeating "that human" to tie similar words together.

Signals the end of the explanation; includes "why," a small mistake the speaker makes.

"Well, there's, there's multiple components to innovation, but the innovation, the way I describe it is, it's the end result of that human creativity, that human ingenuity. The ability to come up with ideas is, is a skill anybody can apply, but what separates the people from really the innovators is, is people who actually execute the ideas. They translate that creativity and that passion and the ideas they come up with into something that's meaningful, meaning it actually ships, it's a product, it's a service, it's a, it's a non-profit to help people. Whatever it is, it actually gets implemented and that's why, that's how I define innovation."

Suggests that you need to listen for more than one idea about innovation.

"The people" are contrasted with "the innovators"; "people" means "everyone else."

The repetition of the signalling phrase "it's a" adds more emphasis than simply saying "it's a product, service or non-profit."

B. Which main points do you retain from the excerpt? Write a one-sentence summary.

_____

_____

C. Based on the excerpt, what do you think is the most likely question that was asked by the interviewer?

_____

_____

D. Working with a partner, take turns reading the excerpt aloud. Usually, when speaking, we stress content words more and function words (such as *it's* and *into*) less. As you read to your partner, stress some of the repeated words and phrases. Can your partner tell which words are being stressed? Do the stressed words make the passage sound more convincing? (See the Focus on Speaking on page 15 for more on adding emphasis when speaking.)

E. Listen to Phil McKinney's comments on innovation and compare his speech with your and your partner's readings of it.

LISTENING ❶

How to Be Innovative in Your Business

Competition in business is often fierce. Even large companies are likely to fail if they do not innovate. Businesses spend millions on observing consumer behaviour, researching and getting feedback from consumers on products and services. Then, after they make changes to products or processes, they repeat the cycle.

Before You Listen

In this interview, Phil McKinney, a former vice-president and chief technical officer at the computer company Hewlett-Packard (HP), talks about innovation and shares some personal examples of how he conducted product research to find out why consumers were not choosing some HP products.

Think of two similar products you recently considered buying. What factors influenced you to choose one over the other?

_____

_____

Imagine you work at a company selling a product or service, such as a productivity application (app) or a cable television package. The company has many competitors. How would you conduct research to find out why consumers *aren't* choosing your product or service?

_____

_____

_____

In the following excerpt, McKinney mentions obstacles that prevent creative people from innovating. Read the excerpt and reword these obstacles as advice to people who wish to innovate. Use short, simple imperative sentences.

"What tends to hold people back—there's highly creative people—but what tends to hold them back is, is: one is that personal drive, commitment to actually be an innovator; two the self-doubt, 'Oh, someone's not going to like my idea; it's really not all that great of an idea.' Then the third is, is getting out of your comfort zone. Innovation is about change and doing something different, right? The first time I recorded a podcast, I felt like a fool sitting in this bathroom because it was the only quiet room in the hotel to try to do this recording with a little cheap, old microphone plugged into the side of a laptop, you know, but if I hadn't started that, then I wouldn't have had the podcast, I wouldn't be where I'm at right now with my book and everything else that's happened."

_____

_____

_____

_____

_____

While You Listen

The first time you listen to the interview, try to get the general idea. Listen a second time to take notes on each segment and to complete the discovery process in the flow chart on the next page. Focus on the main messages and consider whether McKinney's explanations and examples support his main ideas. Listen a third time to check your notes and add details.

SEGMENT	NOTES
Problem with brainstorming	
Killer questions	
Innovation from teamwork	

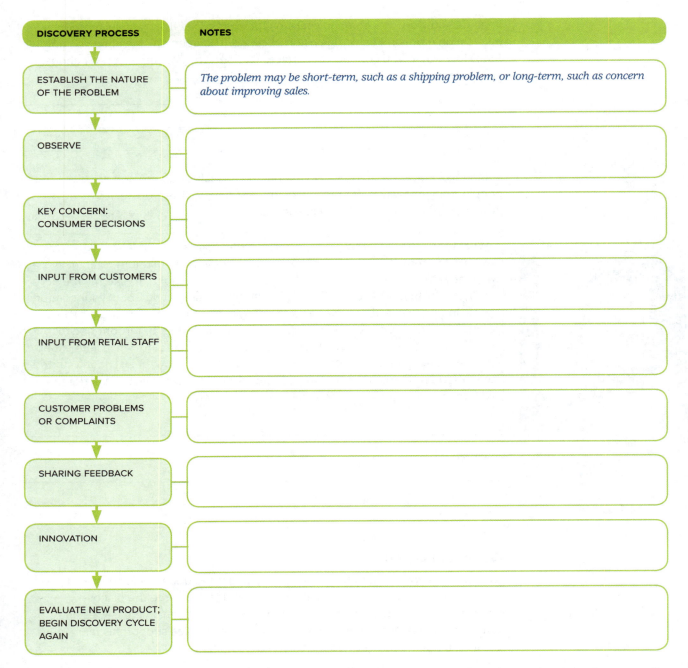

DISCOVERY PROCESS	NOTES
ESTABLISH THE NATURE OF THE PROBLEM	*The problem may be short-term, such as a shipping problem, or long-term, such as concern about improving sales.*
OBSERVE	
KEY CONCERN: CONSUMER DECISIONS	
INPUT FROM CUSTOMERS	
INPUT FROM RETAIL STAFF	
CUSTOMER PROBLEMS OR COMPLAINTS	
SHARING FEEDBACK	
INNOVATION	
EVALUATE NEW PRODUCT; BEGIN DISCOVERY CYCLE AGAIN	

After You Listen

Review your notes and discuss the answers to the following questions in a group.

- Do you agree with McKinney's views on brainstorming?
- Would you say you think more innovatively on your own or in a group?
- Consider the ways in which McKinney fueled innovation at HP by trying to understand consumers' reluctance to buy HP products. Do you think his methods were effective?
- Do you think such methods are an efficient use of a senior manager's time?

WARM-UP ASSIGNMENT
Critique a Product or Service

At the heart of any business innovation is a deep understanding of a product or service. Many innovations begin with the simple question, "How could I make this better?" In answering the question, it's important to look at every aspect of the product or service, define problems from different viewpoints and imagine what could be improved upon. Sometimes an improvement creates something completely different. For example, the delivery of music through digital online services rather than physical recorded formats is a far greater innovation than moving from a record to a cassette tape to a compact disc.

A. Think of a product or service that is popular but that hasn't changed in a long time. Choose something you are familiar with and can critique in a five-minute presentation. Examples might include:
- a home or school appliance
- a mode of transportation
- a common tool
- a service for choosing, buying, ordering or using something

 Visit the Companion Website to learn more about common citation and referencing guidelines.

B. Research the history of your chosen product or service. Pay particular attention to any criticisms you might find. Use at least one online source (other than *Wikipedia*) and one source from the library. Keep complete records of each source, following the citation style preferred in your field of study.

C. Use your research to answer the following questions about the product or service on a separate sheet of paper. Explain each answer, if applicable.
1. Is the product or service too expensive?
2. Is it too slow?
3. Is it inefficient?
4. Is it of poor quality?
5. Is it unattractive?
6. Is it boring?
7. Is it unnecessary?
8. Are there other criticisms? If so, what are they?

D. Prepare your critique using the presentation structure on the next page and adapting notes as necessary. Point out the problems using the actual object or one or two computer slides. Keep short notes on cue cards as a reminder of your key points, but don't write out your whole speech.

PRESENTATION STRUCTURE	NOTES
Greet the audience and introduce yourself and the purpose of your talk.	… and today I'd like to share a critique of …
Briefly explain the product or service.	I'm sure you're familiar with … It was invented by … and has been used for … years. Its purpose was …
Make the transition to the product or service's faults, sign-posting what you will be talking about. "Signposting" means giving an indication of what is coming in a speech so the audience knows what to listen for. (See the Focus on Speaking in Chapter 8 on page 159.)	However, [product/service] has [number] problems. I'd like to go through them one at a time and then open the discussion to questions and comments.
Begin with the first point of your critique, identifying the problem and giving an explanation of it.	The first problem is … This problem is due to …
Continue with the other points. Use separate cue cards to list them.	The second problem …
	The third problem …
	The fourth problem …
	The final problem …
Summarize and ask for questions.	Now, to summarize, I talked about [number] problems … I hope you understood my points and I'm sure you have questions and comments.

E. Present your critique to the class. Take note of any questions, comments and suggestions; they will be useful for the Final Assignment.

VOCABULARY BUILD

A. Below are key words and phrases you will hear in Listening 2 and Listening 3. Check the words you understand. Then, check the words you use.

	UNDERSTAND	USE		UNDERSTAND	USE
agrarian feudal society (n.)	☐	☐	meritocracy (n.)	☐	☐
atrophy (n.)	☐	☐	mobilized (v.)	☐	☐
city states (n.)	☐	☐	modus operandi (n.)	☐	☐
deer in the headlights (n.)	☐	☐	nation state (n.)	☐	☐
divvy up (v.)	☐	☐	orchestrate (v.)	☐	☐
economic meltdown* (n.)	☐	☐	paradigms* (n.)	☐	☐
industrial capitalism (n.)	☐	☐	pillars of society (n.)	☐	☐
investigative journalism* (n.)	☐	☐	Protestant Reformation (n.)	☐	☐
legitimate (adj.)	☐	☐	status* quo (n.)	☐	☐
mainstream media* (n.)	☐	☐	transparency (n.)	☐	☐

*Appears on the Academic Word List

B. Write a definition for each of the words or phrases you do not understand, using a dictionary and continuing on a separate sheet of paper if necessary.

WORD/PHRASE	DEFINITION

C. *Modus operandi* and *status quo* are two Latin phrases often used in English conversation. Match each of the Latin words and phrases to its English definition. Look up the words or phrases you do not know.

LATIN WORD/PHRASE	ENGLISH DEFINITION
1 ad hoc	_____9_____ in itself
2 ad nauseam	_____ for each day
3 bona fide	_____ in exactly the same words
4 carpe diem	_____ for this purpose
5 ergo	_____ in good faith
6 et al.	_____ therefore
7 et cetera	_____ seize the day
8 per diem	_____ something given in exchange for a favour, gift
9 per se	_____ continuing senselessly or to a disgusting degree
10 quid pro quo	_____ the other way around
11 verbatim	_____ and other people
12 vice versa	_____ and other things

D. Complete the following paragraph, using words and phrases from task A.

In an _____, people survived by growing food and making the things they needed. But as business and trade flourished, _____ were founded; eventually, these developed into countries and the _____ became the norm. However, if you listen to _____ today, it seems international trade among the world's economic blocs has become more important than nation states. With this shift, there is the threat that an _____ in one country might bring widespread damage to others. Whether or not this is a _____ concern, it's clear that the _____ of _____ are changing, and innovators will need to look for new ways to _____ decreasing resources among peoples.

E. Discuss the paragraph in task D with a partner. Think about the future of business. Will it all be conducted online? Will new models emerge? What innovative paths can you foresee? Write a paragraph explaining your ideas. In your paragraph, use at least seven words or phrases from tasks A and C.

_____

_____

_____

_____

_____

_____

_____

Visit the Companion Website to complete a vocabulary review exercise for this chapter.

LISTENING ❷

Rebooting Business and the World

The term *rebooting* was first used to describe restarting a computer system. However, it's now applied to restarting other systems, such as ways of doing

business, often with the idea of a new beginning. In this interview, business executive, author and consultant Don Tapscott talks about how a new economic model can reboot business and the world for the digital age.

Before You Listen

Answer the following questions and then discuss your answers with a partner. Think about your answers while you listen to the interview.

Traditional newspapers and magazines are rapidly transforming or disappearing. What business model have they been operating under (i.e., how did they make their money) and why has this model changed?

_____

_____

_____

_____

_____

Hierarchies—with levels of company presidents, managers and workers—have always been important in business, but meritocracies, in which people are valued (and paid) for their ideas, have recently gained ground. Why?

_____

_____

_____

_____

_____

Like new business models, technologies often change the world. One example is the printing press, invented around 1440. Prior to this, most books were handwritten and scarce. How is the Internet similar to the printing press? How is it different?

_____

_____

_____

_____

_____

The following excerpt is from the introduction of the interview, in which Tapscott talks about one of his previous books, *Wikinomics*. As you read the excerpt, use what you learned in the Focus on Listening (page 5) to identify the key word that represents the most important idea.

> "Well, *Wikinomics* was really about the deep structure and architecture of the corporation, and how the Internet radically drops collaboration and transaction costs, and that enables us to orchestrate capability differently in society, to innovate, to create different services and to compete. And it discussed these new models of collaborative innovation in mass collaboration where collaboration can now occur on an astronomical scale."

Summarize the excerpt by rewriting it, using the key word that you have identified as your starting point.

_____

_____

_____

_____

_____

_____

Tapscott mentions the following names and terms during the interview. Do a quick search to identify the ones you don't recognize.

Sibos: _____

Lehman: _____

Jaron Lanier: _____

GreenXchange: _____

Bretton Woods: _____

Kiva: _____

Ushahidi: _____

Snowmageddon: _____

Read interviewer Justin Fox's questions in the first column of the While You Listen table and try to predict what Tapscott's answers might be.

While You Listen

Listen the first time for the general idea and to compare your predictions to Tapscott's answers. Listen a second and third time to take notes and add details.

QUESTIONS	NOTES
Don, you and your co-author, Anthony Williams, wrote a very successful book a few years back called *Wikinomics*. What's happened since then? Why *Macrowikinomics*?	
So is everything going "wiki?" Is all activity gonna go through mass collaboration?	
... in the book you also discuss, at some length critics, like Jaron Lanier is one you give a lot of space to—his critique that the hive mind of the open source world destroys individuality. Is he onto something?	
And so from the perspective of a corporation that's trying to figure out how to navigate this world, how do you go about deciding what to be open source about, what to keep more close to the vest, how to structure these things?	

QUESTIONS	NOTES
... you were already starting to discuss the state and civil society. What are the roles that remain for the nation state and what should move more to this, sort of, open collaboration model?	
... and going to the individual, actually, it's clear that there's a lot of empowerment and, sort of, new ways to make an impact for individuals in this new kind of world. But there are also big questions about how to make a living. So how are we supposed to get paid?	

Chief Executive Officer (CEO), Chief Financial Officer (CFO), Chief Information Officer (CIO), Chief Technology/ Technical Officer (CTO)

After You Listen

Choose one of Fox's questions (other than the first one) and write your own answer, reflecting on your notes and agreeing or disagreeing with Tapscott.

_____

_____

_____

_____

_____

_____

_____

_____

FOCUS ON SPEAKING

Adding Emphasis with Intonation and Stress

Speakers add emphasis to their words, using intonation and stress. Intonation is a musical concept and involves changing the pitch of your voice, raising or lowering it to add emphasis. For example, when you ask a yes/no question in English, you usually raise the pitch of your voice at the end of the sentence. Stress is the energy, or amount of breath, you put into a word. More stress is used for more important words. A pause in speech does not technically add stress to a word or idea, but it does help to draw attention to it.

A. Punctuation marks such as commas, dashes and periods signal pauses in speech. Consider this unpunctuated sentence; add the missing punctuation and underline the words you would stress.

But as the senior manager or CEO of that company I don't delegate innovation activity just to them it's my job

B. Identifying key points and finding ways to stress them when you speak can help listeners follow your talk. Read the following sentences, from Listening 2 and Listening 3, aloud to yourself. Add punctuation and underline the words you think should be stressed.

1 Innovation is at the heart of economic development and it's one of the core features of successful companies worldwide

2. And it discussed these new models of collaborative innovation in a mass collaboration where collaboration can now occur on an astronomical scale

3. I sit in my office I ask clever questions and they're not going to go very far when it comes to innovation

4. And they don't just do that once but they do it systematically to the point that they get this huge innovation premium

5. We've seen in the past the dot-com bubble is there a danger that there might be an innovation bubble in the stock prices

6. You walk into those senior management teams and these organizations that are incredibly innovative and they don't delegate innovation to somebody else

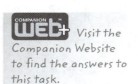 *Visit the Companion Website to find the answers to this task.*

C. Now listen to the original sentences on the Companion Website and compare your answers to them.

The DNA of the World's Most Innovative Companies

DNA (deoxyribonucleic acid), found in each cell of all living organisms, contains the organism's genetic code. When this concept is applied to a company, it refers to the organizing principles that make that company successful. Increasingly, the ability to foster innovation is a key component (i.e., part of the DNA) of a company's success. In this interview, Hal Gregersen, senior affiliate professor of leadership at INSEAD, an international graduate business school, talks about innovative personalities and companies. He explains that studies of twins have shown that genetics accounts for about 25 to 30 percent of our innovation skills, but the rest of our ability to innovate is learned.

Before You Listen

Read the following excerpt in which Gregersen uses Steve Jobs (1955–2011), co-founder and former CEO of Apple, as an example of an innovator. (Note: Gregersen was speaking before the death of Steve Jobs and before Mihalis "Mike" Lazaridis left Research In Motion [RIM].)

"Innovators are people who behave differently and don't just think differently. So, in other words, if I want to be like Steve Jobs and have this capacity to think differently, the fundamental message of innovator's DNA is, people have to behave differently. And so if we walked into Steve Jobs' world and walked around with him, and followed him during a day, we could see him behaving in ways that will generate new ideas. So he observes the world really carefully, he talks to all different kinds of people, he's more than willing to engage in different kinds of experiments, constantly peppering the world and the people around him with questions that provoke people and challenge the status quo. And when Steve Jobs, or anybody else behaves that way—acts differently, asks lots of questions, observes like an anthropologist, experiments constantly, networks for ideas—they're likely to get incredibly insightful ideas about new businesses, new products, new services, breakthrough processes—things that will make a difference for any company."

Based on the excerpt, complete the following recommendations for becoming an innovator.

Behave _____

Observe _____

Talk _____

Engage _____

Pepper _____

Network _____

To "pepper someone with questions" is to ask many questions.

Read the recommendations again and compare them with advice given to would-be innovators in Listening 1. (See Before You Listen on page 7.) Which advice would you follow? Discuss your answer with a partner.

Skim the list of companies in the first column of the While You Listen table and look up those you or your partner don't recognize.

While You Listen

In the interview, Gregersen discusses the innovation of eleven companies. While you listen, take notes on what he has to say about each company and a few of the personalities who work there. Listen again to add notes and examples.

COMPANY	NOTES
Amazon (amazon.com)	*CEO Jeff Bezos …*
Research In Motion	*CEO Mike Lazaridis of RIM (maker of the BlackBerry) …*
Intuit	*CEO and founder Scott Cook …*

COMPANY	NOTES
Bain & Company	*Chairwoman Orit Gadiesh …*
Credit Suisse	*Their Holt division does sophisticated analysis and has an algorithm to calculate the proportion of their cash flow that is set aside for existing versus future products.*
Salesforce.com	
Forbes	
Intuitive Surgical	
Keyence Corporation	
Sony	
Natura	

After You Listen

How do the individuals and companies mentioned by Gregersen fit with the recommendations for becoming an innovator in Before You Listen? Discuss your answers with a partner.

Academic
Survival Skill

Presenting a Project Proposal

Tied to the idea of innovation is a project proposal. Project proposals are not used just in business; they are also important in science, politics and many other fields. At the heart of a project proposal is a need to kindle listeners' curiosity about making something better while overcoming their natural resistance to change. Listeners need to be convinced that an innovative idea will improve a product or a service by clearly addressing an existing problem or need. When you present a project proposal—particularly one that introduces an innovative idea—you are giving a persuasive speech, but often you are also asking for input from your listeners to make your idea better.

A. Consider this approach to presenting a project proposal that outlines an innovative idea. Read the guidelines and the scenario and, on a separate sheet of paper, take notes on what you would say at each step.

PROJECT PROPOSAL GUIDELINES	SCENARIO
AUDIENCE: It's important to know the backgrounds of the people you are presenting to and what role(s) they will play in evaluating and supporting your innovation. If you are presenting to the organization you work for, it's usually best to meet with some of your audience beforehand, to explain your product or service and to get feedback on what could be improved.	*Imagine your audience is made up of community members from a small town, particularly people who use the town library.*
PROBLEM OR NEED: Before presenting your idea, it's important to explain the existing problem or need. Sometimes the problem or need is local (e.g., how to dispose of used light bulbs in an eco-friendly way); sometimes it is international (e.g., problems in poor countries caused by the lack of public lighting after a natural disaster).	*Funding cuts need to be made in the small town. One area that has been targeted is the town library. The number of people who use the library has been decreasing and the building sits on valuable land.*
INNOVATION: Explain your innovative idea, showing how it can solve the problem you have outlined. If your innovation is a product, it might be helpful to create a model of it. If your innovation is a service, consider a role play or flow chart to clearly demonstrate your idea.	*Your innovation is to have library members in the community store the books. Then, when a member wants to read a specific book, he or she will find out who has it and e-mail that person to arrange to get it. The book doesn't need to be returned; the next member who wants it will contact the last person who read it. There might even be a few drop-off spots around town, such as local coffee shops.*
TARGET MARKET: Identify the market for your product or service, explaining how it will benefit your target market.	*Although members of all ages use the library, young children do so with their parents; therefore teens, young parents and all other adults make up the target market.*
UNIQUE FEATURES: Show how your innovation differs from others. Research other solutions to your presented problem or need and explain how your proposal is new and different. Explain whether you offer an incremental change (i.e., a small improvement) or a complete change (i.e., a completely new solution).	*This innovation is a complete change to the way in which libraries currently operate.*
POTENTIAL DOWNSIDES: Consider and share any problems your innovation plan might present and explain how you would address each one.	*Books may be lost or damaged and there would no longer be any staff to find or repair them. It may be inconvenient for people to arrange to meet or drop off books at a designated area.*
STEPS TO IMPLEMENTATION: Explain the steps and resources necessary to realizing your innovation and delivering it to the target market.	*First, the community needs to be educated about the new system. Second, everyone needs e-mail access.*
MEASURES OF SUCCESS: Offer potential indicators of success for the innovation. If the product or service becomes a reality, how will you know if it is successful or not?	*One true measure of success would be if readership increased among library members and people started adding their own books to the original collection.*
LISTENER SUPPORT: Ask your audience for something. It may be feedback, approval for the idea, or financial or other support. If you have presented two or more innovative solutions to the problem or need, you might ask for the audience's preference. Answer any questions your listeners might have.	*An alternative would be to sell all the library books to pay for e-readers for everyone in town and for digital copies of the books.*
THANKS: Thank the audience and encourage members to contact you later if they have additional questions or ideas.	*Share your contact information and the deadline for receiving comments.*

B. With a partner, discuss the scenario and your ideas on how to present it. Compare and contrast ideas and solutions at each step.

C. Take turns with your partner to practise delivering the project proposal. As your partner speaks, take notes on what you see as flaws in the proposal. Discuss these together and look for solutions.

FINAL ASSIGNMENT
Propose an Innovation

Working in a group of three, use everything you have learned in this chapter to prepare and deliver a project proposal of up to fifteen minutes, that outlines a product or service innovation.

A. In the Warm-Up Assignment on page 9, each member of your group critiqued a product or service. Now it's time to consider an innovation that would overcome the flaws of one of these. As a group, choose the product or service you would consider to be the most promising for innovation.

OUR PRODUCT OR SERVICE: _____

PROPOSED INNOVATION: _____

B. Speak with your teacher. Ask for approval of your topic and advice on how to develop it.

C. Do your research. Find out as much as possible about your product or service and add to the criticisms raised in the earlier task. Remember to keep complete records of each source, following the citation style preferred in your field of study.

D. Prepare your project proposal. Use the following table to organize your notes. Refer to the guidelines and your earlier notes from the Academic Survival Skill. If you are presenting a product, consider making a model to give the audience a general idea of its appearance. If you are presenting a service, consider acting out a role play using your service or providing a flow chart to show the steps and options involved.

PROJECT PROPOSAL GUIDELINES	NOTES
AUDIENCE	
PROBLEM OR NEED	
INNOVATION	

PROJECT PROPOSAL GUIDELINES	NOTES
TARGET MARKET	
UNIQUE FEATURES	
POTENTIAL DOWNSIDES	
STEPS TO IMPLEMENTATION	
MEASURES OF SUCCESS	
LISTENER SUPPORT	
THANKS	

E. Once you've prepared your presentation, divide the presenter responsibilities among the members of your group. Practise your presentation together.

F. Present your project proposal to the class. Remember to smile, use positive body language and keep eye contact with your audience.

"Creativity is thinking up new things. Innovation is doing new things."
—Theodore Levitt, economist and Harvard Business School professor (1925–2006)

CHAPTER 2

The Business of Helping Others

Would you like to change the world and somehow make it better? **Countless individuals and organizations are passionate about injustices in the world and have found ways to do something about them.** People with an understanding of business models are often in a position to help make change happen by applying their professional expertise: they become informed, clearly identify a problem, plan a way to address that problem and find the people and the resources to achieve their goals. Maybe you could do this, too. Maybe this is the year you will help change the world.

In this chapter, you will

- listen to and watch presentations on business ethics, fighting illiteracy and supporting small businesses;

- learn vocabulary related to ethics, education, business and economics;

- reflect on listener expectations of a speech;

- practise using rhythm and structure effectively when speaking;

- learn how to present numerical data;

- practise speaking individually, in pairs and in groups;

- give an elevator pitch and prepare and deliver an appeal.

GEARING UP

A. Look carefully at the diagram below. What would be an appropriate title for this diagram? Discuss your answer with a partner.

TITLE: _____

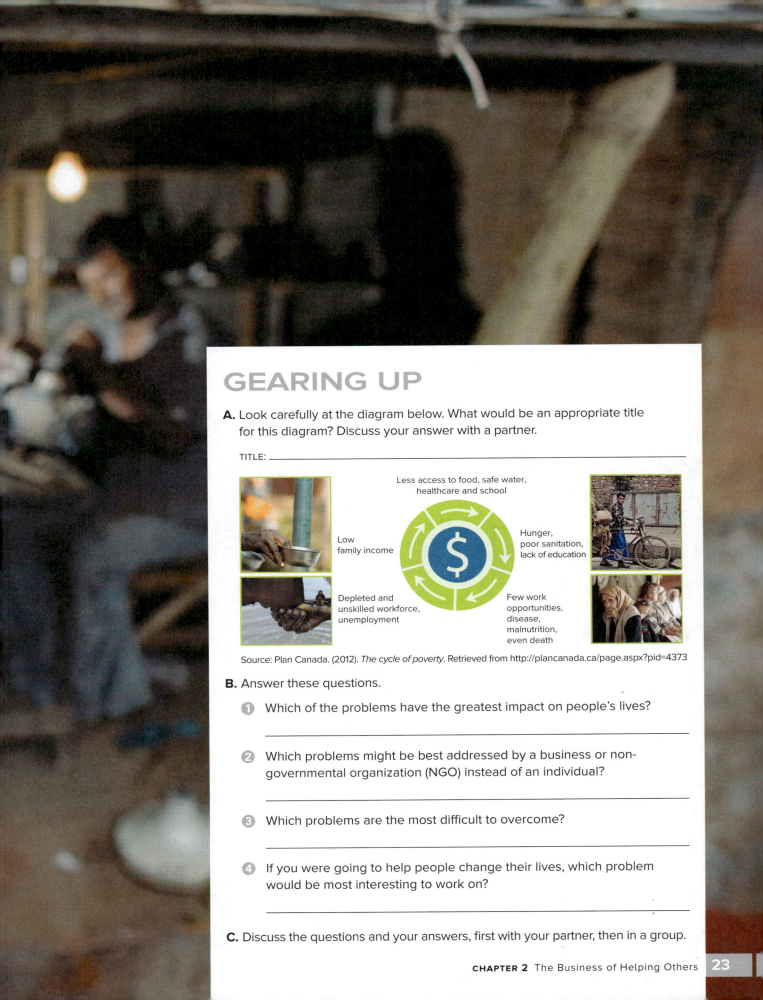

Less access to food, safe water, healthcare and school

Low family income

Hunger, poor sanitation, lack of education

Depleted and unskilled workforce, unemployment

Few work opportunities, disease, malnutrition, even death

Source: Plan Canada. (2012). *The cycle of poverty*. Retrieved from http://plancanada.ca/page.aspx?pid=4373

B. Answer these questions.

1. Which of the problems have the greatest impact on people's lives?

_____

2. Which problems might be best addressed by a business or non-governmental organization (NGO) instead of an individual?

_____

3. Which problems are the most difficult to overcome?

_____

4. If you were going to help people change their lives, which problem would be most interesting to work on?

_____

C. Discuss the questions and your answers, first with your partner, then in a group.

A. Below are key words and phrases you will hear in Listening 1. Check the words you understand. Then, check the words you use.

	UNDERSTAND	USE		UNDERSTAND	USE
acquainted (adj.)	☐	☐	observantly (adv.)	☐	☐
antiquated (adj.)	☐	☐	philanthropy (n.)	☐	☐
callous (adj.)	☐	☐	quotidian (adj.)	☐	☐
culpability (n.)	☐	☐	rapacious (adj.)	☐	☐
dimension* (n.)	☐	☐	recession (n.)	☐	☐
introspection (n.)	☐	☐	reputational (adj.)	☐	☐
intuition (n.)	☐	☐	shareholders (n.)	☐	☐
juxtaposition (n.)	☐	☐	societal expectations (n.)	☐	☐
malevolent (adj.)	☐	☐	tangible (adj.)	☐	☐
nuances (n.)	☐	☐	unprecedented* (adj.)	☐	☐

*Appears on the Academic Word List

B. Write a definition for each of the words or phrases you do not understand, using a dictionary and continuing on a separate sheet of paper if necessary.

WORD/PHRASE	DEFINITION

C. Many adjectives are *ameliorative* (having a positive meaning) or *pejorative* (having a negative meaning). Consider the following adjectives and then place each along a continuum, from the most pejorative to the most ameliorative. When you have finished, discuss your placements with a partner.

antiquated	**AMELIORATIVE**	_____
callous	↑	_____
enduring		_____
informed		_____
malevolent	**NEUTRAL**	_____
motivated		_____
quotidian		_____
rapacious	↓	_____
sophisticated		_____
supportive	**PEJORATIVE**	_____

D. The expression *societal expectations* refers to how most people think others should behave. Write a paragraph outlining what you believe should be society's expectations of behaviour toward the disadvantaged. In your paragraph, use at least five words or phrases from task A.

_____

_____

_____

_____

_____

_____

_____

_____

E. Working in a small group, read and discuss your paragraphs. Look for *consensus*, or agreement.

FOCUS ON LISTENING

Identifying Your Expectations of a Speech

When you are about to listen to a speech, you will probably have some expectations regarding what you are likely to hear, as well as reasons to be interested or not. These expectations are based on what you know about the speaker, the topic and your own purpose for listening.

A. Consider the sources of expectations and their explanations as listed in the first and second columns of the table on the next page. Then, with a partner, discuss the answers to the questions in the third column, relating them to Listening 1.

SOURCE OF EXPECTATION	EXPLANATION	QUESTIONS
YOUR REASON FOR LISTENING	You may be listening because you have been told to, or you may be listening because you are interested in the topic. Defining your reasons allows you to get the most from a speech. Do you expect to learn something new? If so, what do you expect to learn?	Does the title of Listening 1, "The Seven Deadly Sins of Business Ethics," appeal to you? Why or why not? What might you expect to be told about?
SPEAKER'S BACKGROUND	If the speaker represents an organization with a stake in the topic, you may expect the speech to be slanted toward one point of view. A recognized expert might be expected to give a more balanced view.	In Listening 1, how might the speaker's background (she is a consultant on corporate reputation) influence your expectations of what she will say?
TOPIC	The title of the presentation may give a clue to the topic and the objectives, although some titles are purposely vague, to attract attention.	What do you expect the speaker's objectives will be?
CONTEXT	The context includes the place of the speech (e.g., a classroom, lecture hall or stadium), the people who are attending and the general reason for addressing the people present. Are they there to be taught, to be entertained, or to be swayed by new ideas, products or services?	What difference does the context of this talk (a meeting of the Ethical Society) make to your expectations of this speech?
DURATION	In a speech of ten minutes, the speaker has to get to the main point quickly, while a speech of an hour or more can be expected to cover several topics.	Based on the title and the context, how long would you expect the full speech to be?

B. With your partner, discuss how changing the title, context or duration might affect a listener's expectations of a speech. Give examples.

LISTENING ① The Seven Deadly Sins of Business Ethics

Ethical decisions are based on your understanding of what is right and wrong. As a consumer, you make countless ethical decisions every day, such as choosing to buy a cup of coffee from a coffee shop chain (perhaps supporting big business), or going to a small independent coffee shop. Of the two, which business offers workers better pay and benefits? Do you buy a higher-priced fair trade coffee so coffee bean growers are paid a better price? Do you take your own cup to avoid adding disposable cups to landfills? A morning coffee may seem like a small decision with limited consequences, but when a critical mass of people think in the same way, they can shape how businesses and governments conduct themselves.

Before You Listen

Listening 1 deals with a corporate interpretation of the weaknesses traditionally called the "seven deadly sins": envy, gluttony, greed, lust, pride, sloth and wrath. The speaker, Linda Locke, points out that these sins are typified in an old television series, *Gilligan's Island*, in which each of the characters could be said to represent a different deadly sin.

Give an example of how each of the seven deadly sins might be committed in business. When you have finished, compare your examples with those of a partner.

SIN	EXAMPLE IN BUSINESS
ENVY	
GLUTTONY	
GREED	
LUST	
PRIDE	
SLOTH	
WRATH	

Here is the second paragraph of the talk you will listen to. It indicates the speaker's general tone: her attitude and emotional connection to the subject and the audience. A speaker's tone can range from playful and entertaining to indignant and angry. What does the paragraph suggest to you about the tone of the speech? What reasons would the audience have for listening to it?

> "So, at first, the question is: is the idea of sin relevant in 2011? It may seem antiquated to many people because it's not a concept perhaps here, at the Ethical Society, that we think about every day. Now as a young Catholic girl, I went to church every week to confess my two sins. They were stealing candy from my sister and talking back to my mother, every week. Clearly I suffered from either a lack of creativity or a lack of introspection."

_____

_____

_____

_____

_____

While You Listen

The first time you listen, try to get the general idea. Listen a second time to take notes on each segment. Focus on the main message and consider whether the explanations and examples support the speaker's main ideas. Listen a third time to check your notes and add details.

SEGMENT	NOTES
So, who among you recognizes the names ...	
So, at first, the question is: is the idea of sin relevant in 2011?	
But it seems to me the idea of sin is at the centre of our public conversation.	
But, by definition, a sin is behaviour that is unethical.	
Reputation is the set of judgments made by others ...	
In the 1990s, studies of perceptions of major institutions suggested that people trusted corporations ...	
Starting in 2007, after centuries of building an industry based on trust, the US financial services industry ...	
In the mid-90s, Shell Oil was surprised by the simultaneous public outrage ...	
Today, no company should be surprised by public disapproval of its actions.	
Now, boardrooms are generally ruled through logic ...	
The dimension that interests me the most ...	

SEGMENT	NOTES
Society, it seems, is deciding to trust a company based on quality but …	
The creator of *Gilligan's Island* understood the universality of perceptions regarding ethical issues.	
Now, why do we care about these sins?	
The first is greed. We all know greed as a sin of excess.	
I've read that the world's major faiths have no such illusions about greed.	
People get caught up in a culture that is fast-paced and make decisions that, in retrospect, were unwise.	
Now, for another take on greed—and pride and sloth—let's consider pharmaceuticals.	
Now, why would companies knowingly release a drug with harmful side effects?	

After You Listen

Look at the examples of sins in business that you wrote in Before You Listen. Has listening to "The Seven Deadly Sins of Business Ethics" changed any of your ideas? Discuss other examples with your partner and add these to your answers.

VOCABULARY BUILD

A. Below are key words and phrases you will hear in Listening 2 or Listening 3. Check the words you understand. Then, check the words you use.

	UNDERSTAND	USE		UNDERSTAND	USE
advocate* (v.)	☐	☐	infrastructure* (n.)	☐	☐
blue-chip (adj.)	☐	☐	interventions* (n.)	☐	☐
business model (n.)	☐	☐	intractable (adj.)	☐	☐

▶

	UNDERSTAND	USE		UNDERSTAND	USE
creditworthy* (adj.)	☐	☐	marginalized* (adj.)	☐	☐
cumulative* (adj.)	☐	☐	non-negotiable (adj.)	☐	☐
endowment (n.)	☐	☐	proposition (n.)	☐	☐
ethics (n.)	☐	☐	synergy (n.)	☐	☐
flagship program (n.)	☐	☐	theoretical constructs* (n.)	☐	☐
foundation* (n.)	☐	☐	transitioned (v.)	☐	☐
guarantor* (n.)	☐	☐	vis-à-vis (prep.)	☐	☐

*Appears on the Academic Word List

B. Write a definition for each of the words or phrases you do not understand, using a dictionary and continuing on a separate sheet of paper if necessary.

WORD/PHRASE	DEFINITION

C. Acronyms are words formed by joining the first letters of a term or name, such as *scuba* (self-contained underwater breathing apparatus). Initialisms are abbreviations in which each letter is pronounced individually, such as *MIT* (Massachusetts Institute of Technology). The speakers in Listening 2 and in Listening 3 use these two types of abbreviations. Find the full form of each acronym or initialism from the fields of business and international aid and write a short explanation of the term. Search online or use a dictionary.

ABBREVIATION	FULL FORM	EXPLANATION
B2B	*Business to Business*	*businesses working with each other, rather than for the public*
BMW		
CAMFED		
CEO		
ICT		
NASDAQ		
NGO		
VC		

D. Listening 2 and Listening 3 also contain several business terms. Use these terms to complete the paragraph that follows.

advocate	business model	endowment	~~foundation~~	marginalized
blue-chip	creditworthy	flagship program	guarantor	non-negotiable

Our _____*foundation*_____ has been very fortunate to receive a large _____ from a wealthy family who owns one of the country's largest _____ investment companies. Our objective is to help _____ women in the developing world who have been unable to get work because of a lack of education or training. Although we _____ several approaches, our _____ is providing women with pedal-operated sewing machines. These women are not _____ and have no one to act as a _____ for any loans they might try to get. Our _____ is to give them the sewing machines and money to buy some cloth and thread. The only _____ part of our agreement with the women is that they may not sell their sewing machines.

E. Discuss the paragraph in task D with a partner. Does this seem like a good business model? Why should the women not be able to sell their sewing machines? What other ideas would you implement to make the business model more effective? Write a paragraph explaining your ideas. In your paragraph, use at least seven words or phrases from task A.

_____

_____

_____

_____

_____

_____

_____

_____

 Visit the Companion Website to complete a vocabulary review exercise for this chapter.

LISTENING ❷

Bringing the Power of Education to Children around the World

In 1998, John Wood, then an executive with Microsoft, was trekking in Nepal and was invited to visit a rural school. He was shocked to find that the school had only a few books—mostly inappropriate novels and travel books thrown away by backpackers. With the help of friends, Wood collected 3,000 books and returned to the school, carrying the precious load on the backs of eight donkeys. The delight on the children's faces changed his life. Since then, Wood has made it his goal to work with others to build schools and libraries and to promote education across the developing world.

Before You Listen

The introduction of the interview with Wood gives some statistics about Room to Read's cumulative accomplishments in the developing world in 2008. In the table on the next page, the last column shows more recent accomplishments. Use these figures to discuss with a partner how Room to Read grew in the intervening years.

The developing world is made up of countries with low standards of living and little industry; these countries score poorly on the Human Development Index.

ACCOMPLISHMENTS	2008	2012
Access to enhanced educational opportunities	1.7 million	6.7 million
New schools	440	1,556
New bilingual libraries	5,200	13,599
Long-term scholarships for girls	4,000+	17,810

Source: Room to Read. (2012). OurPrograms Retrieved from http://www.roomtoread.org/

In 2008, ...,
but by 2012, ...

Compare these classrooms to each other and to those of your own childhood. What differences can you see?

_____ _____

_____ _____

_____ _____

_____ _____

_____ _____

While You Listen

In this interview, Wood talks about the various activities of Room to Read and how these activities are financed. Read the excerpts. Then, listen to the interview and take notes on the activities and on the different ways Wood has been able to find financial and other support.

EXCERPT	NOTES
And so I started funding some very small projects, like libraries in Nepal ...	
I was very fortunate that I had met a gentleman named Dinesh Shrestha in Nepal, ...	

EXCERPT	NOTES
The book, *Leaving Microsoft to Change the World*, has been really great for Room to Read in terms of ...	
The other big growth for Room to Read has come in our school program. We have now opened, about 725 schools is our estimate ...	
So, we're heavily reliant on private capital. We don't take government funding.	
And we're so proud of the corporate, the blue-chip corporate funders we have.	
People like Don Valentine, the founder of Sequoia Capital. He and his wife, Rachel, ...	
People like Jeff Skoll and his team at the Skoll Foundation, people like Bill Draper and Robin Richards Donohoe and Jenny Schilling Stein at the Draper Richards Foundation ...	
She said to her students, "Being poor is no excuse for not being generous. Even if you can give a penny, that's going to mean something."	
I had a student last week come up to me in Calgary, where I was speaking at a 400-person businessman's lunch, ...	

Xenophobia is made up of the Greek words for "stranger" and "fear." Today it refers to a hateful attitude toward foreigners and immigrants.

After You Listen

Wood also talks about the impact even a small amount of money can make in improving the lives of students around the world. What do you think are the most effective ways of supporting education in the developing world?

_____

_____

_____

_____

_____

_____

_____

WARM-UP ASSIGNMENT
Give an Elevator Pitch on Supporting a Good Cause

The term *elevator pitch* comes from the idea of selling an idea to an investor in the time it takes an elevator to go from the lobby to the top floor of a building, anywhere from thirty seconds to a few minutes. Research and present a three-minute elevator pitch to an investor or a philanthropist. Talk about a problem in the developing world and your solution to it. End with a direct appeal for investment or for a donation. Focus on a project where just a little money could help make a big difference.

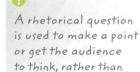
A. Choose a topic:
- access to clean water
- access to education
- access to food
- access to medical care
- access to shelter

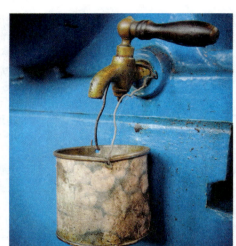

B. Do your research. Find one source online (other than *Wikipedia*) and one source in the library. Keep complete records of each source of information, following the citation style preferred in your field of study.

C. Structure your elevator pitch. Start by giving background information. If applicable, use dates and statistics. Speak from the general to the specific. If you are having difficulty getting started, you can work with some of the following ideas and phrases.

- Ask a rhetorical question that reveals the problem to your audience.

  "When you get a glass of water from the tap, do you ever think how miraculous running water would seem to some people in the developing world?"

- Outline the problem.

  "Since [date], [large number] people have died because of ..."

  "One key problem that keeps people in poverty is ..."

  "The problem of _____ is most severe in [specific region or country] ..."

- Explain one or more specific solutions.

  "The cost of giving each person a year's worth of ..."

  "The only thing necessary to solve the problem is ..."

  "With only $ _____, a family could ..."

- Make a direct appeal. Ask your audience to invest or to donate something such as money, time, expertise or materials, so you can take action.

  "I'd like to ask you to give just ... for a new ..."

  "I want you to donate ... so we can ..."

D. Present your elevator pitch. Don't read from your page. The speech is short enough that you should need only a single cue card listing your key points.

Using Rhythm and Structure Effectively

One of the characteristics of a good speech is the use of rhythm. In 2005, Nelson Mandela (1918–) gave a short speech in which he talked about eliminating poverty in the developing world. This excerpt shows his use of rhythm and structure to create an emotional and compelling message.

A. Read the excerpt to yourself and then read it aloud. Underline words and phrases that add force to Mandela's message. Then, summarize Mandela's speech in one or two sentences.

> "But in this new century, millions of people in the world's poorest countries remain imprisoned, enslaved and in chains. They are trapped in the prison of poverty. It is time to set them free. Like slavery and apartheid, poverty is not natural. It is man-made and it can be overcome and eradicated by the actions of human beings. And overcoming poverty is not a gesture of charity. It is an act of justice. It is the protection of a fundamental human right, the right to dignity and a decent life. While poverty persists, there is no true freedom."

> ! *Apartheid refers to the white South African government-approved racist laws that discriminated against the country's majority black population between 1948 and 1991.*

_____

_____

_____

_____

_____

_____

_____

B. Look at the excerpt again. Consider how the patterns of words, use of repetition and different sentence lengths help Mandela to add force to his message. Does he make a convincing connection between poverty, on the one hand, and slavery and apartheid on the other? Why or why not? Discuss with a partner.

Image of poverty created by placing it in direct comparison to prison →

Definition of overcoming poverty strengthened by contrasting what it "is not" with what it "is" →

Circular structure to emphasize the main idea, with the conclusion referring back to the opening image of poverty as imprisonment →

> "But in this new century, millions of people in the world's poorest countries remain <u>imprisoned, enslaved and in chains</u>. They are trapped in the <u>prison of poverty</u>. <u>It is time to set them free</u>.
>
> Like slavery and apartheid, poverty is not natural. It is man-made and it can be overcome and eradicated by the actions of human beings.
>
> And overcoming poverty <u>is not</u> a gesture of charity. <u>It is</u> an act of justice. <u>It is</u> the protection of a fundamental human <u>right, the right</u> to dignity and a decent life.
>
> While <u>poverty</u> persists, there is no true <u>freedom</u>."

← *Sequence of expressions with similar meanings to add force*

← *Necessary action suggested by a short, direct sentence*

← *Longer sentences contrast with short, sharp sentences before and after, to keep audience's attention*

← *Repetition of "right" to add force*

C. Following the explanation of the excerpt in task B, use rhythm and structure to write notes for a short new speech addressing the problem researched in the Warm-Up Assignment.

STRUCTURE	NOTES (EXAMPLES)
• Identify the problem and use repetition to make your point. • Use a vivid image, metaphor or symbol that captures the listener's attention.	Like _____, _____ is a problem that …
• Explain the action to address the problem. • Explain that a solution is possible. • Expand on your ideas. Use sentences of various lengths.	But we can change this …
• Remind readers what the problem is not and what it is.	The [problem] is not _____; it is _____!
• Expand on the problem and the solution. Use multiple arguments to add force.	A solution is possible; it will simply take …
• Offer a concluding statement that reinforces your opening statement.	Remember: the most important thing is …

Reference

Mandela, Nelson. (2005). Speech in London's Trafalgar Square for the campaign to end poverty in the developing world. BBC News. Retrieved from http://news.bbc.co.uk/2/hi/uk_news/politics/4232603.stm

LISTENING ③

Poverty Is a Threat to Peace

Alfred Nobel (1833–1896) became enormously wealthy through his many inventions, including dynamite, as well as from his ninety arms factories. Shortly before his death, he tried to make up for the pain weapons had produced and established Nobel Prizes for the sciences, literature and peace. In 2006, Muhammad Yunus (1940–), an economics professor from Bangladesh, was awarded the Nobel Peace Prize for his work establishing the practice of microcredit loans that has allowed countless people to raise themselves out of poverty.

Before You Listen

What do you know about microcredit loans—loans of a few dollars that give the poor enough capital to start a small business? An example might be a loan to buy a few ducks whose eggs could be sold. Discuss microcredit loans with a partner and how a small amount of money could be used to start a business.

In the Focus on Listening (pages 25–26), you learned how certain aspects of a speech can raise expectations in the listener. Here is an excerpt from Yunus' acceptance speech. Read and discuss it with your partner. What expectations does Yunus' introduction create for you, the listener? What might you expect the rest of the speech to be about?

"[Ladies and gentlemen,] by giving us this prize, the Norwegian Nobel Committee has given important support to the proposition that peace is inextricably linked to poverty. Poverty is a threat to peace.

"World income distribution gives a very telling story. Ninety-four percent of the world income goes to 40 percent of the world population, while 60 percent of people live on only 6 percent of world income. Half of the world population lives on two dollars a day."

While You Listen

In Yunus' acceptance speech, he often refers to dates and statistics. The first time you listen, try to fill in as much of the missing data as you can. Use the second listening to check your answers and to fill in any that you missed the first time. Listen a third time to take notes on Yunus' message.

Yunus' speech
World leaders gathered at the United Nations, in _____, and adopted, among others, a historic goal to reduce poverty by half, by _____.
But then came _____ and the Iraq war, and suddenly the world became derailed from the pursuit of this dream.
Till now, over _____ has been spent on the war in Iraq by the USA alone.
The creation of opportunities for the majority of the people—the poor—is at the heart of the work that we have dedicated ourselves, during the past _____ years.
In _____, I found it difficult to teach elegant theories of economics in the university classroom, in the backdrop of a terrible famine that was raging in Bangladesh.
When my list was complete, I had the names of _____ victims who borrowed a total amount of US $_____.
That was when I decided to create a separate bank for the poor. I finally succeeded in doing that in _____. I named it Grameen Bank or Village Bank.
Today, Grameen Bank gives loans to nearly _____ million poor people; _____ of them are women. In _____ villages of Bangladesh, Grameen Bank gives collateral-free income-generating loans ...
Since it introduced them in _____, housing loans have become, have been used to construct _____ houses.
In a cumulative way, the bank has given a total of _____ billion dollars.
The repayment rate is _____.
Financially, it is self-reliant and has not taken donor money since _____.
Deposits and own resources of Grameen Bank today amount to _____ of all outstanding loans.

According to Grameen Bank's internal survey, _____ of our borrowers have crossed the poverty line.

It is _____ years now since we began.

One of the _____ decisions developed and followed by them are to send children to school.

Grameen Bank now gives _____ scholarships every year.

There are _____ students on student loans.

Over _____ students are now added to this number annually.

In Bangladesh, _____ of the poor families have been reached with microcredit.

We are hoping that by _____, all _____ of the poor families will be reached with microcredit.

There are now _____ beggars in the program.

About _____ of them have already stopped begging completely.

Typical loan to a beggar is only $_____.

Today, there are nearly _____ telephone ladies providing telephone service in all the villages of Bangladesh.

Grameen Phone has more than _____ subscribers and is the largest mobile phone company in the country.

... the telephone ladies, they generate _____ of the revenue of the company.

Out of the _____ board members who are present here today, _____ are telephone ladies.

Telenor owns _____ share of the company; Grameen Telecom owns _____ .

Social business is important because it addresses very vital concerns of mankind. It can change the lives of the bottom _____ of the world population and help them to get out of poverty.

Each hospital will undertake _____ cataract surgeries per year at differentiated prices to the rich and the poor.

NOTES

After You Listen

Which of the numbers and dates are most memorable? Why? Review your notes and think about what else you have heard on this topic. Summarize the main facts and ideas in Yunus' speech and share them in conversation with your partner.

_____

_____

_____

Academic
Survival Skill

Working with Statistics

The use of statistics can add weight to a presentation, but how often have you listened to a speech full of numbers and come away confused or unable to remember the details? When using statistics as part of a speech, you need to ensure that the way you present the numerical data is clear and relevant and therefore has the maximum impact on your audience.

A. When you present numerical data, you can express it in different ways. Choosing to do so in fractions (1/5th), percentages (20%) or in expressions (one in five) can affect your audience's perceptions of the importance of the number. Fill in the missing figures and words in the following table.

FRACTION	PERCENTAGE	WRITTEN EXPRESSIONS
1/5	20%	one-fifth 20 percent one in five
1/4		
1/3	33%	
1/2		
2/3	66%	
3/4		
97/100		almost all ...

B. Statistics often seem boring and meaningless. Consider these figures: Canada's rate of relative child poverty is 13.3 percent, which ranks the country twenty-fourth of thirty-five industrialized countries. (UNICEF, 2012)

Now consider the same information presented in a way that gives it more force.

> What do these industrialized countries have in common? Luxembourg, United Kingdom, Estonia, New Zealand, Slovakia, Australia, Hungary, Belgium, Malta, France, Germany, Ireland, Switzerland, Czech Republic, Austria, Sweden, Denmark, Slovenia, Norway, Netherlands, Cyprus, Finland, Iceland. Here's the answer. In every single one of them, children are better off than they are in Canada. Fourteen percent of children in Canada—that's one in seven children—are living in poverty. We can do better.

The rhetorical question at the beginning of the paragraph prompts you to think, and the list of countries is like a riddle that you have to solve.

Even though you cannot be expected to remember the names of all the countries, you are given a stronger impression that Canada is far below international standards.

Read the following statement and rewrite it to make it more memorable.

> The USA ranks thirty-fourth out of thirty-five countries in terms of child poverty, with 23.1 percent of children living in a household in which disposable income, when adjusted for family size and composition, is less than 50 percent of the national median income. The thirty-fifth country is Romania. (UNICEF, 2012)

_____

_____

_____

_____

_____

C. It is often difficult for people to imagine numbers without comparisons to more easily imaginable times or quantities. Consider the following statistics about the 2011 earnings of the wealthiest and poorest people in the world.

> In 2011, the International Monetary Fund estimated that the average income of a person living in Qatar was US $102,943. The average income of a person living in the Democratic Republic of the Congo was US $348. (IMF, 2012)

Consider another way of expressing the same data.

> On average, a worker in the Democratic Republic of the Congo would have to work more than 295 years to earn the yearly income of a person living in Qatar.

Now read the following excerpt from Yunus' speech and consider the statistics. Find a way to express them so that they are more memorable. For example, consider comparing the cost of a typical loan to what you might normally spend twelve dollars on. Then, rewrite the excerpt on a separate sheet of paper.

> "Three years ago we started an exclusive program focusing on the beggars. None of Grameen Bank's rules apply to them. Loans are interest-free; they can pay whatever amount they wish, whenever they wish. We gave them the idea to carry small merchandise such as snacks, toys for the kids or household items for the housewives, when they went from house to house for begging. The idea worked. There are now 85,000 beggars in the program. About 5,000 of them have already stopped begging completely. Typical loan to a beggar is $12."

References

International Monetary Fund (IMF). (2012). World economic and financial surveys: World economic outlook database. Retrieved from http://www.imf.org/external/pubs/ft/weo/2012/01/weodata/index.aspx

UNICEF Innocenti Research Centre. (2012). Measuring child poverty: New league tables of child poverty in the world's rich countries. United Nations Children's Fund (UNICEF). Retrieved from http://www.unicef-irc.org/publications/660

FINAL ASSIGNMENT
Deliver an Appeal

Now it's your turn. Use everything you have learned in this chapter to research and deliver an appeal of up to fifteen minutes.

A. From the Nobel website (www.nobelprize.org), choose an organization that has won the Nobel Peace Prize, and prepare an appeal. The purpose of your appeal is to outline the aims and achievements of the organization in order to convince a sponsor to donate money to cover the initial publicity and set-up costs of your branch.

ORGANIZATION: _____

TARGET SPONSOR: _____

B. Speak with your teacher. Ask for approval of your choice of organization and target sponsor and advice on how to develop your appeal.

C. Do your research. Find interesting details about your organization from at least three sources, including the organization's website. Keep complete records.

D. Plan your presentation. Use the following table to organize your notes.

PRESENTATION STRUCTURE	NOTES
Consider the challenges facing your organization and ask a rhetorical question that relates those challenges to your sponsor.	
Outline the challenges in detail. Cite statistics, but look for ways to convert the numbers into ideas that will be more meaningful to your sponsor.	
Explain one or more general solutions that have been undertaken by your organization. Celebrate the successes while emphasizing that work still needs to be done.	
Make a personal appeal. Ask your sponsor to take action, in this case by donating money, goods or services to help establish a local office/chapter.	
Thank your sponsor and allow time for questions. Be sure to have references to support your facts and statistics in case you are asked about them.	

E. Support your speech. Consider how a computer-based presentation could help you better illustrate your key points.

> "You have not lived today until you have done something for someone who can never repay you."
> —John Bunyan (1628–1688)

CRITICAL CONNECTIONS

In Chapter 1, you learned of businesses and individuals who foster innovation and, in Chapter 2, you considered ways of helping the disadvantaged. However, not all attempts at aid and innovation end happily. Now, you have the opportunity to put together everything you've learned and think critically to complete integrated tasks.

1. Ghanaian economist Dr. George Ayittey has described international aid in Africa using a quotation commonly attributed to Albert Einstein (1879–1955): "Insanity is defined as doing the same thing over and over again and expecting different results." How do you think this quotation applies to models of military, economic and humanitarian international aid? Discuss with a partner.

2. What innovative approaches to aid might solve some of the problems you have raised above, in task 1? Discuss your questions and answers in a group. Select your best answers and share them with the class.

3. Consider the following case study:

> In the 1980s, Norway built a fish-processing plant on the shores of Lake Turkana, Kenya, to help economically disadvantaged local tribespeople who suffer during frequent droughts. However, the local people are nomadic livestock herders. The multi-million dollar plant today sits vacant.

Research the case study and prepare for a class discussion on the following questions.

- What should have been done before Norway spent millions building the fish plant?

- What is one innovative use to which the fish plant might now be put?

- What might be an innovative project that would help the Turkana tribespeople in future?

In your discussion, persuade others with facts and statistical data. Rephrase your statistics to show how they compare and contrast with other statistics. See the Academic Survival Skill on page 40 for help. Consider the problem or need, your project and its unique features and potential downsides, steps to implementation, measures of success and support you might want.

COMPANION WEB+ Visit the Companion Website for new content related to Chapters 1 and 2.

CHAPTER 3

Machines in Your Future

The Greek historian Herodotus (484–425 BCE) wrote of a prisoner who escaped his chains by cutting off his foot, later using a wooden substitute in its place. It's the first written record of an artificial limb. Since then, scientists and doctors have researched ways to replace limbs, bones and organs, including the skin. Implant technology has been used to compensate for problems in sight and hearing as well as to automatically regulate the heartbeat. Now, research is going further, raising questions about how new technologies might make us stronger, faster and smarter. Cyborgs—creatures that are part human, part machine, with abilities that far exceed our own—have long been part of science fiction. **However, with medical and technological advances, stories of cyborgs are becoming less about fiction and more about science.**

In this chapter, you will

- listen to interviews about experimental implants, personal robots and future enhancements;

- learn vocabulary related to engineering, medicine and ethics;

- learn how to use definitions and explanations to clarify concepts;

- practise asking different types of questions;

- learn how to work with Likert scales;

- practise speaking individually, in pairs and in groups;

- research and explain a technical subject and prepare and deliver a presentation with a partner.

GEARING UP

A. Consider the diagram. Then, answer the questions that follow.

First artificial implants into humans

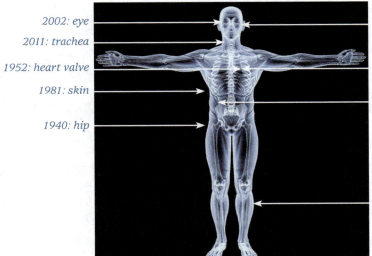

2002: eye
2011: trachea
1952: heart valve
1981: skin
1940: hip

1970s: cochlear implant
1969: heart
1958: pacemaker
Pending: liver
1964: body-powered limb

① Besides heart valves, the pacemaker and the artificial heart, what do you think are the three most important implants (among those labelled on the diagram) for improving quality of life?

_____

② What natural abilities of other animal species, such as breathing under water, might you want to have? Why?

_____

_____

③ If you were to get an implant that would improve your natural abilities—for example, an artificial eye to see things at great distances—what would you choose? What side effects might result?

_____

_____

B. Discuss your answers, first with a partner, then in a group.

A. Below are key words and phrases you will hear in Listening 1. Check the words you understand. Then, check the words you use.

	UNDERSTAND	USE		UNDERSTAND	USE
Alzheimer's (n.)	☐	☐	manifest (v.)	☐	☐
clinical trials (n.)	☐	☐	neurons (n.)	☐	☐
cochlear implants (n.)	☐	☐	pacemakers (n.)	☐	☐
degeneration* (n.)	☐	☐	Parkinson's disease (n.)	☐	☐
electrode (n.)	☐	☐	peripheral (adj.)	☐	☐
electromagnetic power (n.)	☐	☐	photoreceptors (n.)	☐	☐
enhancement* (n.)	☐	☐	regulation* (n.)	☐	☐
genetic defects (n.)	☐	☐	sonar (adj.)	☐	☐
infrared (adj.)	☐	☐	Tourette's syndrome (n.)	☐	☐
lab rat (n.)	☐	☐	ultrasonic (adj.)	☐	☐

*Appears on the Academic Word List

B. Write a definition for each of the words or phrases you do not understand, using a dictionary and continuing on a separate sheet of paper if necessary.

WORD/PHRASE	DEFINITION

C. Alzheimer's disease, Parkinson's disease and Tourette's syndrome refer to three medical conditions named after the researchers who first described them. Match each condition to its definition. Look up the ones you do not know.

CONDITION	DEFINITION
❶ Hodgkin's lymphoma, described in 1832 by pathologist Thomas Hodgkin	_____6_____ form of autism
❷ Addison's disease, described in 1855 by physician and scientist Thomas Addison	_____ adrenal gland disorder
❸ Huntington's chorea, described in 1872 by neurologist George Huntington	_____ illness caused by a bacterium in raw or undercooked food
❹ Salmonellosis, described in 1885 by the team of veterinary surgeon Daniel Elmer Salmon	_____ cancer of the lymphatic system
❺ Crohn's disease, described in 1932 by three physicians including Burrill Bernard Crohn	_____ neurodegenerative disorder
❻ Asperger's syndrome, described in 1944 by pediatrician Hans Asperger	_____ inflammatory disease of the digestive system

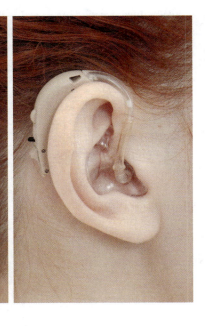

D. Complete the following paragraph, using words and phrases from task A. Where necessary, make singular nouns plural to fit the sentence.

In 2004, the World Health Organization estimated that more than 275 million people had moderate to profound hearing loss. Some people are born deaf due to _____; others become deaf through accidents or, particularly in older people, through a natural _____ of hearing. Fortunately, new technologies such as _____ use _____ to activate _____ in the ear to restore some hearing. In addition, _____ are under way to find _____ to regular hearing. Imagine improving your hearing so that you could eavesdrop from greater distances, or even using _____ technology to hear like a bat. Such experiments may pass government _____, but they challenge traditional ethics.

E. Working in a small group, share your answers from task D.

Listening for Definitions and Explanations

Delivering a speech or lecture in front of an audience, or even speaking to a single person, is very different from simply reading aloud. One of the great differences is audience response, which causes a good speaker to adjust the message and offer definitions and explanations when necessary, such as in reaction to puzzled looks from audience members or from the person you are speaking to.

▶

A. Throughout Listening 1, the speakers use a number of methods to offer definitions and explanations to clarify concepts. As you read the following excerpts, consider the different methods of clarification and their effectiveness.

A direct explanation of what the term "cybernetics" means →

"Well, it [cybernetics] is humans and technology linking together."

"This" refers to "brain stimulator" and is followed by an explanation. →

"They implant the deep brain stimulator. This is a long, long electrode—it's actually about four or six electrodes on the end of a long wire, pushed into the centre of someone's brain, into the subthalamic nucleus, a very small part of the brain, and an electrical pulse is applied there to overcome the effects of Parkinson's disease."

← *The phrase "it's actually" signals a more detailed explanation of a brain stimulator.*

← *The phrase, "a very small part of the brain" is set off with pauses (represented by commas) and spoken in a lower pitch.*

The repetition of "neurons" here indicates that "growing" and "culturing" are near-synonyms. →

"I mean, one of the things we have done: growing neurons, culturing neurons, and then linking them up to a robot body."

The phrase after "extrasensory perception" (ESP) is an imperfect explanation; the real meaning of ESP is the latter part of the sentence, not "the idea of plugging myself in." →

"... one of the things that fascinates me the most is the idea of extrasensory perception, the idea of plugging myself in and being able to see or sense things that currently, I can't."

"Well, now the stage is set for the visual equivalent of the cochlear implant, ..."

← *The word "equivalent" signals a comparison, but it doesn't help if you don't know what a cochlear implant is.*

You learn that retinitis pigmentosa is a genetic disease, and genetic disease is defined, but "mixed bag of conditions" doesn't explain retinitis pigmentosa. →

"Retinitis pigmentosa is a genetic disease, so a condition which is passed from generation to generation, and it's kind of a mixed bag of conditions, which are all grouped under the same name."

B. The explanation "a very small part of the brain" in the excerpt is provided in a parenthetical phrase structure (i.e., a phrase set off with commas or dashes). In addition to providing explanations, parenthetical phrases are used to add clarifications or indicate digressions. Combine each of the following pairs of sentences into a single sentence by using a parenthetical phrase. When you have finished, practise saying the full sentences, dropping your pitch for the parenthetical phrases.

1 I built my first robot hand when I was fourteen and won a competition. In 1997, I was fourteen.

   I built my first robot hand when I was fourteen—in 1997—and won a competition.

   _____

2 I built the hand from leftover engine parts and a few things I ordered online. My father worked in a car repair shop.

   _____

   _____

3 First, I replaced the old engine parts with new aluminum ones. The old parts were very heavy.

   _____

   _____

④ My friend's mother suggested I show it to a prosthetics company. She was an electrical engineer.

_____

_____

⑤ The company said they were not interested but invited me to intern with them. The company's name was Limbus Prosthetics.

_____

_____

C. Choose words or phrases from task A of the Vocabulary Build on page 46 and complete each sentence with its definition or an explanation.

① By _____, I mean _____

_____ .

② A _____ is a _____

_____ .

③ _____ refers to _____

_____ .

④ Another way of understanding _____ is _____

_____ .

⑤ The equivalent of _____ is _____

_____ .

⑥ _____ is actually _____

_____ .

D. Share your definitions and explanations with a partner. Discuss which of your partner's examples are the most effective in making the defined concepts clear. Which are the least effective?

LISTENING ①   **Cybernetics and Implants to Improve Impaired Vision**

The term *cybernetics* has its origins in the Greek language and refers to steering or navigation. It relates to the idea of communication and integration between machines and animals, including humans. There are already many cybernetic devices, from cochlear implants for assisted hearing, to insulin pumps that deliver measured doses of the hormone. In the two interviews in Listening 1, Kevin Warwick, professor of cybernetics at Reading University, and Marcus Groppe, academic clinical lecturer at Oxford University's Nuffield Laboratory of Ophthalmology, talk about the future of medical implants.

Before You Listen

Here is one of the opening paragraphs of Warwick's interview. Based on what he is saying, what would you predict will be the focus of the interview? Discuss your ideas with a partner.

> "Well, it [cybernetics] is humans and technology linking together. So, it's the whole system. It's looking at how it all works together, so lots of practical examples, but as you—you've spoken about cyborgs, which is more of a, which has perhaps been more of a science fiction thing in the past, where the technology and the human are integral. They're not separable, as it were, and the abilities, possibly, could be much, much more than humans alone."

Implants and prosthetic devices are increasingly important to improving the lives of people who suffer from various diseases and injuries. Only in recent decades have doctors been able to alleviate some of the disorders associated with blindness by performing cataract surgery and replacing corneas. However, for many, blindness remains untreatable. What are some of the consequences of different degrees of vision loss?

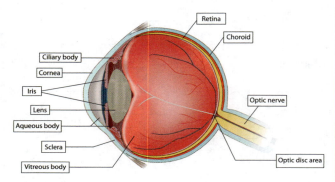

DEGREE OF VISION LOSS	CONSEQUENCES
POOR VISION	
PARTIAL BLINDNESS	
COMPLETE BLINDNESS	

While You Listen

The first time you listen, try to get the general idea. Listen a second time to take notes on the answers to the questions the interviewers ask. Focus on the main messages and consider whether the explanations and examples support the speakers' main ideas. Listen a third time to check your notes and add details.

WHAT IS CYBERNETICS?: INTERVIEW WITH KEVIN WARWICK	
QUESTIONS	NOTES
Perhaps there are things that we might not consider as being sort of cybernetics. Things like pacemakers and cochlear implants—we're quite familiar with that sort of technology. Does that count?	
And what about the more far-off things—things we might actually consider science fiction—really, really mixing machines with people? Where are we at with that kind of thing?	
I have to say that one of the things that fascinates me the most is the idea of extrasensory perception, the idea of plugging myself in and being able to see or sense things that currently, I can't. Where are we with those sorts of areas of cybernetics?	

WHAT IS CYBERNETICS?: INTERVIEW WITH KEVIN WARWICK	
QUESTIONS	NOTES
And how did your brain adapt to having this implant taken out? That must have been quite strange to go back to normal.	
And looking ahead, where are the big challenges that lie ahead of you in terms of all of this research you're doing? Would you say it's the scientific barriers that you have to break through, or is it the ethics actually?	

IMPLANTS TO IMPROVE IMPAIRED VISION: INTERVIEW WITH MARCUS GROPPE	
QUESTIONS	NOTES
... So, can you just fill us in on what retinitis pigmentosa is?	
And their diseases manifest just within those photoreceptor cells that convert the light waves into electrical signals, but presumably, you leave the other structures in the eye, including, critically, the optic nerve, intact?	
So if you can get signals back into them, then you can help them to experience at least some semblance of vision again. Is that your starting hypothesis?	
So, because you've lost the photoreceptors—the bits that see the light—your chip takes the place of those photoreceptors you've lost and then couples itself onto these ganglion cells that make the optic nerve that would transmit that signal into the brain?	
Wow! How big is it then?	
How do you get the chip in, in the first place?	
And how do you power the chip?	
And what data have you got so far that this is going to be a success? The fact that you're going into humans argues that you must have satisfied enormous amounts of regulation and other preliminary data requirements to show that this is likely to work, but how soon do you expect to see results?	
And how many people are you going to do in total? When will you know whether or not you've got a success on your hands? What's the long-term follow-up here?	

After You Listen

Work with a partner and compare your notes. What do you find most surprising? Would you consider receiving implants as Warwick has done?

A. Below are key words and phrases you will hear in Listening 2 or Listening 3. Check the words you understand. Then, check the words you use.

	UNDERSTAND	USE		UNDERSTAND	USE
algorithms (n.)	☐	☐	generative* (adj.)	☐	☐
animatronic (adj.)	☐	☐	inanimate (adj.)	☐	☐
augmented (adj.)	☐	☐	insights* (n.)	☐	☐
autonomous (adj.)	☐	☐	longevity (n.)	☐	☐
avatars (n.)	☐	☐	nanotechnology (n.)	☐	☐
bionic (adj.)	☐	☐	progeny (n.)	☐	☐
biotechnology (n.)	☐	☐	prosthetics (n.)	☐	☐
embodied cognition (n.)	☐	☐	social intelligence (n.)	☐	☐
emotive (adj.)	☐	☐	symbiotic (adj.)	☐	☐
entities* (n.)	☐	☐	synergistic (adj.)	☐	☐

*Appears on the Academic Word List

B. Write a definition for each of the words or phrases you do not understand, using a dictionary and continuing on a separate sheet of paper if necessary.

WORD/PHRASE	DEFINITION

C. The affix *bio-* refers to life and is found in words such as *bionic*, *biotechnology* and *symbiotic*. For each affix in the table, find three words that contain it. Look the words up in a dictionary to ensure their meanings are related to the affix.

AFFIX	MEANING	WORDS WITH AFFIX	DEFINITIONS
sym-	together, united or alike		
nano-	very small or one-billionth		
-oid	having the form of or resembling		

D. In his short story "The Man That Was Used Up," Edgar Allan Poe (1809–1849) describes a war hero who has a dark secret: his entire body, including his tongue, is a series of prosthetics that have to be assembled by his servant. Write a paragraph explaining what sorts of prosthetic devices a person living one hundred years from now might think of as being commonplace. In your paragraph, use at least seven words or phrases from task A.

_____

_____

_____

_____

_____

_____

_____

_____

 Visit the Companion Website to complete a vocabulary review exercise for this chapter.

E. Working with a partner, read and discuss your paragraphs. What is similar in your visions of future prosthetics and what is different?

LISTENING ② Personal Robots

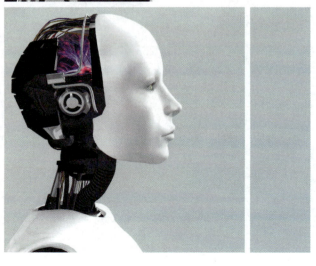

There are millions of working robots in the world today. Most are factory equipment, doing simple jobs such as repetitively welding a few joints on cars or assembling electronics. The future will doubtlessly see more robots in the home, where some are already at work. These include autonomous vacuum cleaners that roam the house cleaning the floor and then return to a wall socket when they sense they need to be recharged. In this interview, Cynthia Breazeal, director of the Personal Robots Group at the MIT Media Lab, explains we are also likely to witness the emergence of robots with social intelligence—robots that act as companions, helping us, and even advising us, when they think our ideas are faulty.

Before You Listen

One issue in the development of robots for personal use is the question of aesthetics. What should they look like? A curious issue is a concept popularized by MacDorman (2005): the *uncanny valley*. The concept refers to feelings ranging from unease to repulsion upon being confronted with something that is almost, but not exactly, human-like. This suggests we would be comfortable with a personal robot companion that either looked perfectly human or human with obvious non-human elements. Describe what you think a personal robot should look like and illustrate your description with a sketch. Give your sketch a title.

An android, sometimes called a humanoid, is a robot with a human appearance.

TITLE: _____

While You Listen

Breazeal and her interviewer, Sabine Hauert, discuss several issues around the social intelligence of robots. After introductory statements, most of the discussion focuses on Leonardo, a robot designed for human interaction. The first time you listen, try to get the general idea. Listen a second time and take notes on the answers to the questions in the following table. Listen a third time to check your notes and add details.

QUESTIONS	NOTES
Who is Rosey the Robot Maid and what human emotions did she have?	
What are some things that personal robots currently do?	
What are Kismet, the MDS humanoid and Leonardo?	
LEONARDO	
How does Leonardo understand people?	

QUESTIONS	NOTES
LEONARDO	
What does Breazeal mean by "mind-reading" or "theory of mind skills"?	
How does Leonardo predict and understand?	
How does Leonardo collaborate or cooperate?	
How does Leonardo show the ability to learn?	
How does Leonardo work with people?	
What does Leonardo *not* look like?	
In essence, how was Leonardo designed?	
What parts of Leonardo are expressive and how does he show these expressions?	
Who is Leonardo more realistic in his behaviour than?	
How does Breazeal describe Leonardo's movements?	
How does Leonardo display social cues?	
How does Leonardo exhibit social behaviour?	
What three kinds of actions does Leonardo anticipate when considering what people are likely to do so that he can help humans achieve their goals?	
How does Leonardo help a person make better choices?	

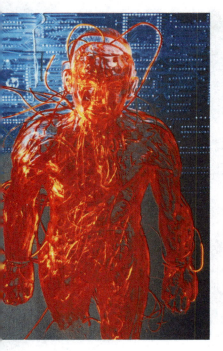

After You Listen

Consider the following quotation in which Rod Grupen, professor of computer science at the University of Massachusetts, claims that the study of robots is very much about learning more about ourselves: "At bottom, robotics is about us. It is the discipline of emulating our lives, of wondering how we work" (quoted in Hapgood, 2008). Relate his comments to what Breazeal has said about her work with Leonardo. When you have finished, share your ideas with a partner.

_____

_____

_____

_____

_____

References

Hapgood, F. (2008). When robots live among us. *Discover Magazine.* Retrieved from http://discover magazine.com/2008/jun/27-when-robots-live-among-us/article_view?b_start:int=2

MacDorman, K.F. (2005). Androids as an experimental apparatus: Why is there an uncanny valley and can we exploit it? CogSci-2005 Workshop: Toward Social Mechanisms of Android Science, 106–118.

FOCUS ON SPEAKING

Asking Questions

Questions can take many forms, and the different types will partly determine the quality of answers you will receive.

A. Read the different types of questions and the examples from the listenings in this chapter. Which questions are the easiest to answer? Which are the most difficult? Rank them from 1 (the easiest) to 7 (the most difficult).

TYPE OF QUESTION	DESCRIPTION	EXAMPLES FROM LISTENINGS	RANK
OPEN	Open questions give listeners the widest possible scope to share what they know.	So, can you just fill us in on what retinitis pigmentosa is?	
CLOSED	Closed questions do the opposite: elicit a specific fact; one of two choices, such as yes or no; or agreement or disagreement.	Is that your starting hypothesis?	
PREFACED	Prefaced questions offer background information before the actual question is posed.	Perhaps there are things that we might not consider as being sort of cybernetics. Things like pacemakers and cochlear implants—we're quite familiar with that sort of technology. Does that count?	
FOLLOW-UP/PROBING	Follow-up/probing questions draw out additional details on a topic.	And how did your brain adapt to having this implant taken out?	
HYPOTHETICAL	Hypothetical questions explore a person's concepts and beliefs by presenting a novel situation and asking how he or she would react or respond.	What might I believe to be true if I were seeing the world from this person's perspective?	

TYPE OF QUESTION	DESCRIPTION	EXAMPLES FROM LISTENINGS	RANK
LEADING	Leading questions give the speaker's point of view and invite agreement or disagreement. They are used when the speaker is trying to persuade the audience or is looking for a strong contrary opinion.	… where are the big challenges that lie ahead of you in terms of all of this research you're doing? Would you say it's the scientific barriers that you have to break through, or is it the ethics actually? I mean, that must presumably throw up a whole lot of issues … part machines and where that's taking us.	
MULTIPLE	Multiple questions group several questions together. Listeners may have to separate them into groups, or even write them out, to be able to address all the component questions.	What does this robot look like and what are its actuators, sensors and computation …?	

B. On a separate sheet of paper, write your own sample questions on a topic related to robots' appearances and functions.

C. Working with a partner, take turns asking and answering your sample questions. Ask follow-up questions. Take notes on your partner's answers.

D. Review your notes on your partner's answers. Which answers met your expectations based on the questions asked? Which were a surprise?

Don't answer an irrelevant question. Instead, say, "I think the real question is …" and then give your answer.

WARM-UP ASSIGNMENT
Research and Explain a Technical Subject

One of the most basic speaking tasks is to explain something new in an informative way. In this assignment, you will need to consider how to communicate the essential aspects of a new technology and present the technical information so that it is easy for an audience to understand.

A. Choose an implant or other technology that is used to treat a medical condition. Refer to the diagram in Gearing Up (on page 45), or consider other implants, such as artificial knees, face transplants or other prosthetic devices used to replace limbs or parts of limbs.

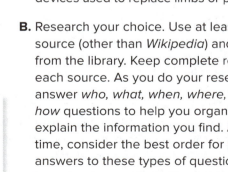

B. Research your choice. Use at least one online source (other than *Wikipedia*) and one source from the library. Keep complete records of each source. As you do your research, try to answer *who, what, when, where, why* and *how* questions to help you organize and explain the information you find. At the same time, consider the best order for providing answers to these types of questions in order to make your presentation as clear as possible. An example, based on the BrainGate implant, has been provided on the next page.

Web+ Visit the Companion Website to learn more about common citation and referencing guidelines.

IMPLANT: BRAINGATE		
QUESTIONS	EXAMPLE	YOUR RESEARCH NOTES
Who invented the implant?	Researchers at Brown University and the University of Chicago built the original version; more recently, Stanford University and other institutions have been continuing its development.	
What is the implant? What is it made of? How does it work?	A tiny sensor is implanted into the brain to record electrical signals; software decodes these signals and translates them into computer commands for physical actions; and a communication device, such as a prosthetic limb, performs the actions.	
When was it invented?	BrainGate has been in development since 2002 and in clinical trials since soon after that.	
Where in the body is it implanted?	BrainGate is implanted in the part of the brain that controls motion.	
Why is the implant necessary? What is it for?	The implant is intended for people who have lost the use of their limbs. It may someday allow paralyzed people to fully control computers, wheelchairs, artificial limbs and other devices.	

C. Prepare a five-minute presentation on your chosen technology. Frame your research with an opening and a closing statement. It's often good to begin with information that is already familiar to your audience.

OPENING STATEMENT	SAMPLE TEXT	EXAMPLES FOR YOUR TOPIC
QUESTIONS	How many of you have (heard about … / know someone who has … / wondered how people with X problem …)?	
PREAMBLE	I'm sure everyone has heard about … In (date), something was invented that changed the lives of (millions) of people.	

CLOSING STATEMENT	SAMPLE TEXT	EXAMPLES FOR YOUR TOPIC
SUMMARY	I'll now review the five main points. I think you'll agree that the benefits of … include …	
INVITATION TO ASK QUESTIONS	Now that you better understand … perhaps you have some questions about ….	

Use similes to help your audience better understand: BrainGate is like having an assistant inside your head.

D. Write key points on cue cards and find visual aids such as an image or example of the technology. You may want to include pictures of people receiving and using the technology in a computer presentation. Practise delivering your presentation in front of a partner.

E. Deliver your presentation to the class.

Ayesha Khanna is managing partner at Urban Intel, founder and director of the Hybrid Reality Institute and director of the Future Cities group at the London School of Economics. Among her many interests are the ways in which technology is changing human behaviour, particularly as we move from implants and prosthetic devices that make us as good as we were before, to innovations that make us better. Is it possible that the future will see a divide in society based on the ability to afford enhancements?

Before You Listen

In the Focus on Listening on page 47, you explored how speakers offer definitions and explanations, often based on audience response. Read the following paragraph, taken from Khanna's interview, and write definitions of the five ages she mentions.

> "To understand the Hybrid Age, we have to at least step back and look at patterns of human-technology interactions and see how we've evolved from the Stone Age—where 250,000 years ago, we were essentially using stone tools to dominate other species—to 10,000 years ago, when we entered the Agrarian Age. Completely different sets of technologies fundamentally changed the way we live our lives. And then 250 years ago, the Industrial Age spawned the era of mass consumerism, mass urbanization, mass production. And then about fifty years ago, we had a number of new technologies which heralded the Information Age: everything from the personal computer to the INTEL chip to what we now know as the World Wide Web and social media. So, in other words, every time the nature of technology changes, our patterns of human technology and interaction—therefore the way the species lives its life—fundamentally changes. So the Hybrid Age is the age that we are entering in now, because technology has once again evolved, and it has become in three ways very different from before. It is now becoming increasingly small and ubiquitous in nature."

STONE AGE: _____

_____

AGRARIAN AGE: _____

_____

INDUSTRIAL AGE: _____

_____

INFORMATION AGE: _____

_____

HYBRID AGE: _____

_____

Discuss your answers with a partner and then discuss other details about each age that you know. Based on what you learned in the Focus on Listening, identify the strengths of Khanna's explanations. How could they be better?

While You Listen

Khanna answers the questions asked by interviewer Nora Young, but she expands her answers to address general topics as well. The first time you listen, try to get the general idea of what Khanna is explaining. Listen a second time and take notes. Pay particular attention to the six questions Khanna raises in her answers to Young. You will need this information in order to complete After You Listen. While you listen a third time, check your notes and add details.

QUESTIONS	TOPIC	NOTES
So you argue that we're now entering something called the "Hybrid Age." What is that, and how is it different from the age that I thought we were in, which is the Information Age?	Technology becoming social	
… I mean, you could argue that humans and machines have a sort of symbiotic relationship—or at least that we need them. Is that what's new, then, in terms of our relationship with machines?	Relationship with machines	
… what do you think some of the challenges are that'll face us as we move into this Hybrid Age?	Hybrid Age challenges	
You talk about the role that biotechnology and nanotechnology will play in our lives. So, can you paint me a bit of a picture? How would an ordinary person experience that, day to day?	Biotechnology Nanotechnology	
… So how do hybrid humans, cyborg humans, factor into your idea of the Hybrid Age?	Hybrid Age	
… It seems to me that in a way, whether you're talking about nanotechnology or cyborgs or pervasive computing, you're talking about a way in which technology has become almost internalized into who we are as people.	Internalized social media	

After You Listen

When Khanna raises questions in her answers to Young, she is mapping out areas for further thought and research. Choose one of her questions and, in a paragraph, write your answer. Then, find others in the class who have answered the same question and compare and discuss your answers.

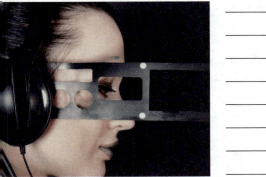

_____
_____
_____
_____
_____
_____
_____
_____

Academic
Survival Skill

Measuring Attitudes with Likert Scales

Collecting data is done in many ways, such as through observation and experiments. Other methods include structured conversations and questionnaires, whose purpose is to collect data on what people think. One of the most common methods of collecting data about attitudes and opinions is to use a Likert scale.

A Likert scale typically includes five answer points; seven- and nine-point scales are sometimes used, but it can be difficult for respondents to understand subtle differences. Regardless of the number, the central point indicates a neutral answer. A Likert scale is most often used to measure a response to a statement in terms of agreement, frequency, importance or likelihood. In the following examples, there is a scale for each item, but it is more common to have a single scale for a series of items.

A. Indicate your response to each of the following. When you have finished, compare your answers with those of a partner.

AGREEMENT

1 In thirty years, almost every home will have a robot working in it.

☐	☐	☐	☐	☐
strongly agree	agree	neither agree nor disagree	disagree	strongly disagree

FREQUENCY

2 I use technology to communicate socially.

☐	☐	☐	☐	☐
very frequently	frequently	occasionally	seldom	never

IMPORTANCE

3 Supplying free prosthetics and technology to help disabled people is ...

☐	☐	☐	☐	☐
very important	important	moderately important	of little importance	unimportant

LIKELIHOOD

4 I check e-mail and other messages when I'm bored.

☐	☐	☐	☐	☐
almost always true	usually true	sometimes true	usually false	almost always false

B. For each of the four term types, write a statement that could be used to measure practices or attitudes surrounding technology.

AGREEMENT

FREQUENCY

IMPORTANCE

LIKELIHOOD

_____

_____

_____

_____

_____

_____

_____

_____

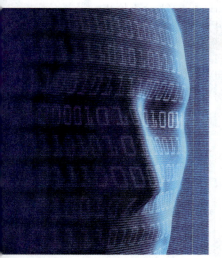

The best way to display and compare Likert scale data is on a bar chart.

C. Likert scale statements can also be used to collect data orally, such as in phone or face-to-face interviews. Read five or more people your statements from task B and, using the answer choices appropriate to each term type, ask for their responses.

D. Summarize the responses from task C and share them with the class, identifying which points have the most and least support.

FINAL ASSIGNMENT
Give a Presentation with a Partner

Working with a partner, use everything you have learned in this chapter to prepare for and deliver a presentation of up to twenty minutes (ten minutes per speaker).

A. Choose a topic related to a possible physical or mental enhancement that would allow people to improve their abilities and/or senses. For example, you might choose x-ray vision, a wireless Internet connection directly to the brain, or prosthetic legs to run faster than the fastest athlete.

OUR TOPIC: _____

B. Speak with your teacher. Ask for approval of your topic and advice on how to develop it.

C. Do your research. Look in the library and on the Internet for current research on your topic. Start by creating a list of related search terms. One resource you might find useful is science fiction stories that suggest ways your chosen enhancement might eventually be used.

D. Together, decide which Likert scale you will use (agreement, frequency, importance or likelihood) and, based on your research, create a questionnaire of at least five statements. Test the questionnaire on one or two classmates to make sure the statements are clear. Then, give the questionnaire to a wider audience of ten or more people. Ask each to indicate his or her responses and return the questionnaire to you. You can do this by distributing printed questionnaires or through e-mail. Alternatively, you might decide to do this face to face, in which case you and your partner should be prepared to follow up with additional questions. (See the different types of questions in the Focus on Speaking on page 56.)

E. Plan your presentation. Use the following table with *who, what, when, where, why* and *how* questions to organize your notes. Present the information generated by the questions in the order that makes the most sense and frame your presentation with opening and closing statements. Decide where and how you can best integrate the data from your questionnaire. Convert the findings from at least one set of answers into a bar chart and use it to support your talk; the best choice of question is one that shows a range of answers. Once you've prepared your presentation, divide the points between you and your partner.

PRESENTATION GUIDELINES	NOTES
OPENING STATEMENT	
WHO	
WHAT	
WHEN	
WHERE	
WHY	
HOW	
CLOSING STATEMENT	

F. Practise your presentation with your partner, and then deliver it to the class.

"Will robots inherit the Earth? Yes, but they will be our children. We owe our minds to the deaths and lives of all the creatures that were ever engaged in the struggle called Evolution. Our job is to see that all this work shall not end up in meaningless waste."
—Marvin Minsky, cognitive scientist in artificial intelligence (1927–)

CHAPTER 4

Creating Sustainable Cities

Imagine placing a huge glass dome over a large city. What would happen? Most cities—and everyone in them—would soon die. On one hand, the city would be deprived of inputs like food, water, fuel and other necessities. On the other hand, without enough trees to convert carbon dioxide to oxygen, or enough space to dispose of liquid and solid wastes, outputs like air pollution and waste would accumulate. **The aim of making cities more sustainable is to preserve and enhance quality of life by making wise use of resources and by minimizing pollution and all kinds of waste,** often through recycling and creative building and urban planning solutions. In doing this, individuals, groups and public officials must change not only a city's environment, but also the attitudes of the people living there.

In this chapter, you will

- listen to a lecture and watch presentations on sustainable urban development;

- learn vocabulary related to sustainability, the environment and urban infrastructure;

- predict questions and answers;

- learn how to moderate a panel discussion;

- interpret charts;

- practise speaking skills individually, in pairs and in groups;

- defend a point of view and participate in a panel discussion.

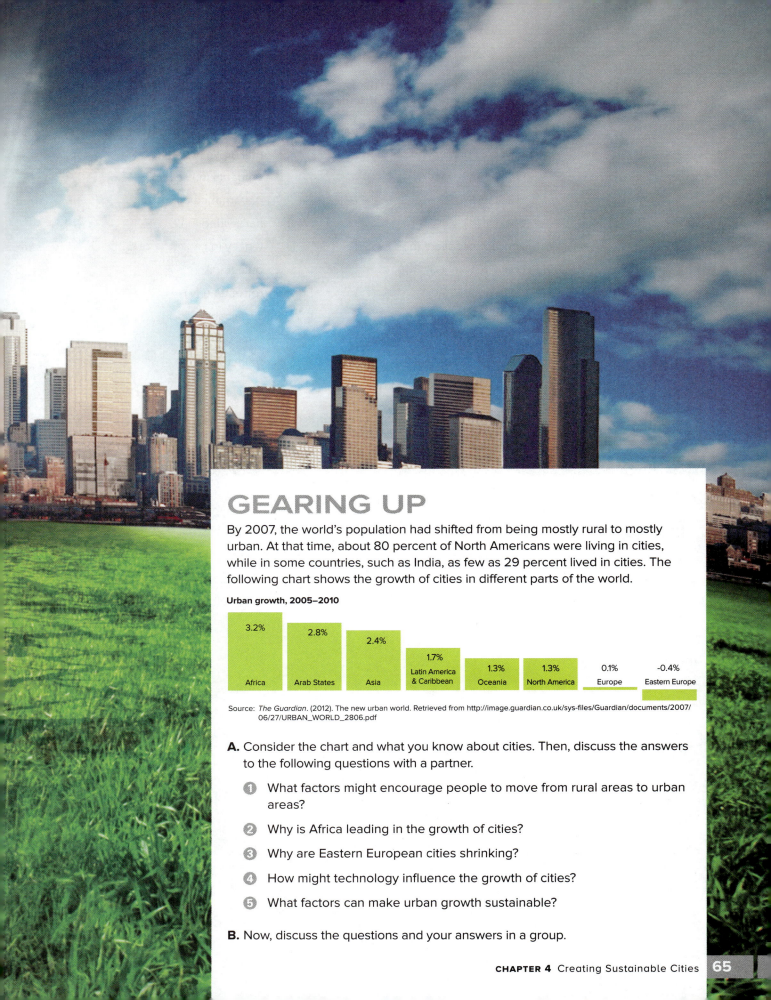

GEARING UP

By 2007, the world's population had shifted from being mostly rural to mostly urban. At that time, about 80 percent of North Americans were living in cities, while in some countries, such as India, as few as 29 percent lived in cities. The following chart shows the growth of cities in different parts of the world.

Urban growth, 2005–2010

Region	Growth
Africa	3.2%
Arab States	2.8%
Asia	2.4%
Latin America & Caribbean	1.7%
Oceania	1.3%
North America	1.3%
Europe	0.1%
Eastern Europe	-0.4%

Source: *The Guardian*. (2012). The new urban world. Retrieved from http://image.guardian.co.uk/sys-files/Guardian/documents/2007/06/27/URBAN_WORLD_2806.pdf

A. Consider the chart and what you know about cities. Then, discuss the answers to the following questions with a partner.

1. What factors might encourage people to move from rural areas to urban areas?

2. Why is Africa leading in the growth of cities?

3. Why are Eastern European cities shrinking?

4. How might technology influence the growth of cities?

5. What factors can make urban growth sustainable?

B. Now, discuss the questions and your answers in a group.

A. Below are key words and phrases you will hear in Listening 1. Check the words you understand. Then, check the words you use.

	UNDERSTAND	USE		UNDERSTAND	USE
built environment* (n.)	☐	☐	drill down (v.)	☐	☐
carbon emissions (n.)	☐	☐	effluents (n.)	☐	☐
civic (adj.)	☐	☐	governance (n.)	☐	☐
cocktail (n.)	☐	☐	hardwiring (n.)	☐	☐
conceptualization* (n.)	☐	☐	legacy (n.)	☐	☐
contextualize* (v.)	☐	☐	outlier (n.)	☐	☐
demographic (adj.)	☐	☐	retrofitting (v.)	☐	☐
depletion (n.)	☐	☐	sustainable* (adj.)	☐	☐
deployment (n.)	☐	☐	temporal (adj.)	☐	☐
disconnections (n.)	☐	☐	trajectory (n.)	☐	☐

*Appears on the Academic Word List

B. Write a definition for each of the words or phrases you do not understand, using a dictionary and continuing on a separate sheet of paper if necessary.

WORD/PHRASE	DEFINITION

C. The exact meaning of many words is often determined by the context. Choose words and phrases from task A that would fit the different contexts of each pair of sentences.

1 a) The _____ of the smooth stone took it skipping across the waves.

b) Increasing levels of pollution are sending some creatures on a _____ to extinction.

2 a) To reach the oil, petroleum companies have to _____ 3,350 metres.

b) We can't take the report summary as fact but instead need to _____ to the initial data.

3 a) To make this _____, the bartender mixes rum, lime and pineapple juice.

b) Years of waste disposal in the ocean, without oversight, has led to a poisonous _____ of substances on the ocean floor.

4 a) The process of _____ circuits in radios has been replaced by printing circuit boards.

b) Curiosity is part of the _____ of our brains.

5 a) _____ of service are common among people who routinely fail to pay their phone bills.

b) For some who deny climate change, there are _____ between what they want to believe and reality.

6 a) The environmental group is holding a rally at the _____ centre, to protest the absence of a composting program.

b) Many people consider voting a _____ duty in a democratic society.

D. One sense of the word *legacy* is the achievements and failures that we hand down to the next generation. Legacies can be abstract, such as attitudes toward justice and the environment, or concrete, such as parks and museums. Write a paragraph outlining what you believe your generation's legacy should be in terms of making the world a better place. In your paragraph, use five key words or phrases from task A to help define your expectations.

_____

_____

_____

_____

_____

_____

_____

Use clarification strategies when you're not sure: "By ..., do you mean ...?"

E. In a small group, read and discuss your paragraphs. What common visions do you share about your generation's legacy?

Predicting Questions and Answers

Whether you're in a class or a coffee shop, it's useful to mentally rehearse questions and answers about what others might say. Anticipating a discussion helps build your listening skills by allowing you to focus on information that doesn't fit your predictions.

A. In the opening statements of Listening 1, Tim Dixon, from the Oxford Institute for Sustainable Development at Oxford Brookes University, uses numbered points to outline what he proposes to talk about. This helps his audience know what to expect and form mental questions and answers about what he might say.

Based on Dixon's opening statements, what questions do you predict he will try to answer, and what answers might he give?

DIXON'S OPENING STATEMENTS	PREDICTED QUESTIONS	PREDICTED ANSWERS
"Firstly, to give an overview of cities and their impact on carbon emissions but also on resource depletion and environmental degradation.	*What is the impact of cities' carbon emissions on the environment?*	*A high-emissions city uses far more resources, in turn creating more pollution.*
Secondly, to look at scale and complexity at the city level—and by complexity I'm talking about that in relation to urban transitions.		
Thirdly, to look a little bit at the theoretical conceptualization of urban transition and how those kinds of framework can help our understanding to project pathways to a more sustainable future.		
Fourthly, to look at some examples of sustainable urban development from around the world, both planned and unplanned.		
And then finally, to look at some of the critical success factors that I think need to be in place for us to move to a more sustainable future."		

B. Discuss your predicted questions and answers with a partner. Where do you agree and where do you differ? Why?

Sustainable Urban Development to 2050

The word *sustainable* refers to methods of harvesting commodities, such as certain fish and trees, to avoid their depletion. In this lecture, Tim Dixon uses concepts of sustainability to explore how planned and unplanned cities can endure and prosper in relation to their environments.

Before You Listen

Think about a city you know. Then, predict how that city might look in the year 2050.

BUILDINGS: _____

_____

_____

TRANSPORTATION: _____

_____

_____

PUBLIC SPACES: _____

_____

_____

RECREATION: _____

_____

_____

QUALITY OF LIFE: _____

_____

_____

Utopian and *dystopian* are two terms often used to describe what future societies, including cities, might look like. A utopian city would be one in which a clean, comfortable environment supports people living together peacefully and happily with everything they need. A dystopian city is the opposite: a city in which the physical, social and cultural environment is seriously degraded and crime is ever-present. Review your predictions with a partner and consider whether each represents a utopian or dystopian view of the future.

While You Listen

Near the beginning of Dixon's presentation, he refers to a graph similar to the one below. While you listen, circle key points on the graph and, in the margin, take notes on Dixon's explanations.

Urban and rural populations, by development group, 1950–2050

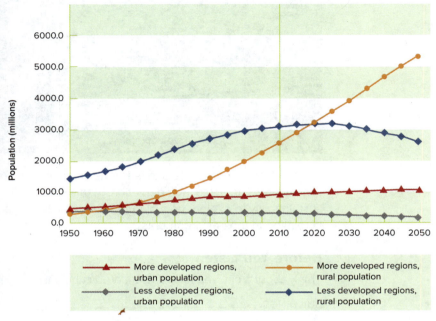

Source: United Nations. (2008). United Nations expert group meeting on population distribution, urbanization, internal migration and development. Retrieved from http://www.un.org/esa/population/meetings/EGM_PopDist/P01_UNPopDiv.pdf

While you listen to the rest of the presentation, complete the flow chart. Write other notes on topics unfamiliar to you on a separate sheet of paper.

TODAY
- 50 percent of the population (3.5 billion people) live in cities

2050
- urban population expected to grow
  by __84__ percent
  or __6.3__ billion people

BUILDINGS CONTRIBUTE
- __20__ percent of water effluents
- __30__ percent of solid waste
- __40__ percent of carbon emissions

BUILDINGS USE
- __10__ percent of land
- __20__ percent of water
- __30__ percent of raw materials
- __40__ percent of energy

CITIES
- global energy consumption: __75__ percent
- carbon emissions: __80__ percent
- Note: Average carbon emissions are lower outside cities; Beijing is a bit of an outlier because data is __outdated__.
  1994-1998

STUDYING CITIES
- new or existing buildings + their _shape + form_
- looking at physical structures _in cities (social + eco uses)_
- looking at individual buildings through to _settlement forms (or regional scales)_

SPATIAL COLLECTIVITY
- complexity of the infrastructure systems within cities as well as the spaces, places and communities that we have; how human form and function relate
- Note: Consider governance, consumption and poverty.

MISMATCHES
- temporal: "It's not in my _term (of office)_."
- spatial: "It's not in my _patch_."
- institutional: "It's not my _business_."

2050
- 350 trillion dollars worth _of investment_
- need for retrofitting cities or re-engineering the buildings and infrastructure
- 80 percent of our _building_ will be present
- only 1 to 2 percent of the buildings in a city are new
- 98 percent of buildings need to be fixed if _we want a sustainable future_

After You Listen

Work with a partner and review the flow chart, comparing your answers. Then, take turns using the boxes like cue cards and explain each one in a conversational way.

VOCABULARY BUILD

A. Below are key words and phrases you will hear in Listening 2. Check the words you understand. Then, check the words you use.

	UNDERSTAND	USE		UNDERSTAND	USE
coalition building (n.)	☐	☐	laundry list (n.)	☐	☐
consensus* (n.)	☐	☐	microclimates (n.)	☐	☐
demographers (n.)	☐	☐	multidisciplinary (adj.)	☐	☐
ecological footprints (n.)	☐	☐	oxymoron (n.)	☐	☐
empirical* (adj.)	☐	☐	pathogens (n.)	☐	☐
hamstrung (adj.)	☐	☐	perfect correlation (n.)	☐	☐
holistic (adj.)	☐	☐	pithy (adj.)	☐	☐
hybrid (adj.)	☐	☐	proponents (n.)	☐	☐
incentives* (n.)	☐	☐	ramifications (n.)	☐	☐
key drivers (n.)	☐	☐	respite (n.)	☐	☐

*Appears on the Academic Word List

B. Write a definition for each of the words or phrases you do not understand, using a dictionary and continuing on a separate sheet of paper if necessary.

WORD/PHRASE	DEFINITION

C. Some terms in Listening 2 and Listening 3, like *laundry list*, have both literal (exact) and figurative (creative) meanings. To understand these terms properly, you need to pay attention to the context because interpreting them literally doesn't always convey the speaker's intention. Research and write literal meanings and figurative uses of the following terms.

	LITERAL MEANING	FIGURATIVE MEANING
1 in the trenches		
2 green roofs		
3 mechanical question		
4 growth machine		
5 common ground		

	LITERAL MEANING	FIGURATIVE MEANING
6 marching orders		
7 lip service		
8 back from the brink		

D. Listening 2 contains terms used to talk about environmentally friendly initiatives. Use these words and phrases to complete the following paragraph.

compost	farmer's market	organic	solar panels
eat locally	green	permeable	waste
ecological footprints	~~infrastructure~~	sewers	water filtration

Just as cities are looking at improvements to their _infrastructure_ to make them more _____, homeowners are increasingly looking at the systems around them to reduce their _____. One of the first places to start, with the biggest impact, is the driveway, which seldom has a _____ surface, so _____ water flows into _____. You might choose to have an _____ garden at home or shop at a local _____ and, when you go out for dinner, to _____. You should also be using your food scraps for _____. Homes themselves can benefit from _____ on the roof and _____ systems that turn grey water from showers and laundry into water for the garden.

E. Which of the green initiatives in task D would be the easiest for you to put into practice and which would be the most difficult? Which initiatives might save you the most money in the long term?

_____
_____
_____

F. Share and discuss your answers with a partner.

COMPANION **WEb+** *Visit the Companion Website to complete a vocabulary review exercise for this chapter.*

Sustainability: The Next Management Frontier, Part 1

Around the world, countless cities are implementing initiatives to improve their environments and make life better for their citizens. Some initiatives, such as regulating use of cars in city centres, are usually top-down decisions by municipal governments. Other initiatives, such as establishing farmers' markets or petitioning for better bicycle paths, are often bottom-up decisions.

Before You Listen

Consider this excerpt from Listening 2, in which Judith Layzer, a professor of environmental policy and planning at MIT, outlines some of the impacts that cities have on the environment and the people who live in them.

"Cities consume three-quarters of the world's resources; they emit about 80 percent of the world's greenhouse gases. They have lots of other environmental impacts as well: they remove nutrients from the landscape, they concentrate waste, they disrupt biogeochemical cycles by disturbing water flows, compacting soils and creating microclimates. More subtly, cities have the psychological effect of removing us from nature so we start to forget that we're really dependent on these systems functioning well for our own livelihoods."

Imagine you are a mayor or city planner. Rank the issues Layzer raises from most important (1) to least important (5).

_____ Cities consume three-quarters of the world's resources and emit about 80 percent of the world's greenhouse gases.

_____ Cities remove nutrients from the landscape.

_____ Cities concentrate waste.

_____ Cities disrupt biogeochemical cycles by disturbing water flows, compacting soils and creating microclimates.

_____ Cities have the psychological effect of removing us from nature so we start to forget that we're really dependent on these systems functioning well for our own livelihoods.

What solutions can you see to some of the problems listed above? Discuss in a group and compare your rankings.

While You Listen

Layzer frames her talk around cities in general and gives examples from specific cities. The first time you listen, try to get a broad sense of what Layzer is talking about. While you listen a second and third time, take notes of examples from each city and how the examples support Layzer's argument that cities are going to help the world become more environmentally sustainable.

CITY	NOTES
Boston, USA	
Chicago, USA	
New York, USA	
Philadelphia, USA	
Curitiba, Brazil	
Berkeley, USA	
San Francisco, USA	
Portland, USA and Seattle, USA	
Toronto, Canada	
Singapore, Republic of Singapore London, UK	
Qingdao, China	
Newark, USA	
Paris, France	

After You Listen

Review the various initiatives that each city is undertaking. Which do you think are the most effective ones for improving a city's sustainability and making it a better place to live? Compare your answers with those of a partner.

_____

_____

_____

WARM-UP ASSIGNMENT
Discuss Two Points of View

There will be occasions when you might be called on to defend a point of view that you don't personally believe in. In this Warm-Up Assignment, you and a partner choose a city and present two different views of how it might evolve by the year 2050.

A. Choose a city both you and your partner are familiar with. Take opposite points of view.

- By 2050, (name of city) will be a utopian paradise.
- By 2050, (name of city) will be a dystopian hell.

B. Research the city, keeping in mind your chosen point of view. Review the initiatives in Listening 2 and research other initiatives that could make your city a utopian paradise, or consider trends and potential problems that could make it a dystopian hell. In your research, look for statistical support for initiatives and trends indicating that things are getting better or worse. Keep complete records of each source, following the citation and referencing guidelines of your discipline.

Visit the Companion Website to learn more about common citation and referencing guidelines.

C. In Listening 1, you already considered changes in buildings, transportation, public spaces, recreation and quality of life. Build on these ideas and investigate inputs such as food, water, energy and other necessities, as well as outputs such as various kinds of waste and pollution. What could happen (e.g., population increase/decrease, technology breakthroughs/breakdowns, famine / new farming innovations) that might affect the sustainability of your city?

D. When you have completed your research, summarize your findings in one or more statements and write your notes on cue cards with details that support your point of view.

E. Taking turns with your partner, present your point of view and supporting arguments to the class.

Moderating a Panel Discussion

When you are interviewing someone, attending a presentation or just making small talk, there are several skills involved in asking and directing questions. These skills are important for showing interest and collecting additional information.

A. In Listening 3, Sarah Slaughter, a lecturer in sustainable business at MIT, acts as moderator and oversees a panel discussion. At different times, she leads the conversation, adds information and directs questions or comments to individual speakers or to the group. As you read the following excerpts, consider the different ways in which Slaughter directs/moderates the discussion.

Restating or summarizing what someone has said is a good way to lead into a new question. You are reminding the audience of what is generally important while focusing on what might be the point or points to follow up on.

"Milton, you've been working with cities around the world."

Sometimes a statement is enough to prompt someone to speak more. If not, ask a follow-up question: "Could you tell us something about …?"

"Well, and as you say, one of the things that's interesting is even just in the last couple of years, there's an organization which lists commercial properties and their recent analysis of the data shows that over the past two to five years, properties that have high energy performance and have reached the LEED rating for the US Green Building Council are actually selling at 10 to 15 percent premiums. And they're getting higher rents …

… So one of the things that we're seeing is the market has been slow to recognize some of these values, but especially with the escalation on the energy prices, we're seeing rapid shifts in the whole market and the market economy in the trade-in quality."

Use your restatement to shift perspectives (e.g., from property owners to the whole market) and shape the conversation along specific lines.

This is a segue from one topic to another. Other expressions used in segues: "which makes me think of …"; "and we can see that in …"; "to follow up on …"

"<u>And that leads to</u> one of the other topics that we touched on briefly in our conversation yesterday, which was as we look at the new generation that's graduating from school …

… And then as you were talking, <u>Bill</u>, in terms of managing teams, one of the things that we had touched on was the degree to which sustainability and particularly the engagement of people's hearts as well as their mind changes some of these issues. <u>Bill, did you want to say something about that?</u>"

When several people are talking, it's important to identify the speaker. Then, you can follow up with an open-ended question for that person.

It's also common to direct questions to a second speaker to get a different perspective (e.g., on jobs in sustainability).

"Well, <u>Judy</u>, you were talking a little bit about the possibility for cities to develop new jobs as they start following industries that are sustainable and things like that. <u>Do you want to talk about that a little bit?</u>"

B. In a small group, formulate a few short statements on the topic of sustainability. Divide the statements among group members. Use key words or phrases from task A of the Vocabulary Build on page 71 in each sentence.

C. Once the class is ready, have the members of your group take turns presenting your statements. A moderator, from another group, will use the skills referred to on the previous page to summarize ideas, ask questions and direct audience questions to your whole group or to individual members.

LISTENING ③   **Sustainability: The Next Management Frontier, Part 2**

This segment is part of the panel discussion that followed Judith Layzer's talk (Listening 2). It involves Layzer and Sarah Slaughter as well as Milton Bevington, of the Clinton Climate Initiative, and Bill Sisson, of the Energy Efficiency in Buildings Project of the World Business Council for Sustainable Development. When you are listening to a panel discussion, it's important to track the questions and comments that drive the presentation.

Before You Listen

Read Slaughter's opening remarks in this excerpt from the panel discussion.

> "So a question I have for the panel is: What is the extent to which sustainability has a competitive advantage, for a specific company, for an organization like a hospital or a university, being able to attract people, or for cities, to be able to attract people to other places?"

As is often the case with people speaking spontaneously, what Slaughter has to say is not particularly clear or concise. On a separate sheet of paper, rewrite Slaughter's opening remarks based on your understanding of what she is trying to say. Break them into specific questions.

Compare your questions with those of a partner and write a final version. Then, try to predict possible additional questions and corresponding answers that might arise from the opening remarks. Work with your partner and take turns asking and answering the questions.

While You Listen

The first time you listen, try to get an understanding of the general topics. Listen a second time to take notes. Focus on what each speaker says in response to the previous speaker, whether there is a direct question or whether they are just building on the previous topic. Listen a third time to check your notes and add details. (Note: Portions of Slaughter's comments are included here to give you a sense of the sequence of the speakers.)

SPEAKER	NOTES
Judith Layzer	
Sarah Slaughter	"Milton, you've been working with cities around the world."
Milton Bevington	
Bill Sisson	
Sarah Slaughter	"Well, and as you say, one of the things that's interesting is …"
Milton Bevington	
Sarah Slaughter	"And that leads to one of the other topics that we touched on briefly …"
Bill Sisson	
Sarah Slaughter	"Well, Judy, you were talking a little bit about the possibility for cities …"
Judith Layzer	
Milton Bevington	
Judith Layzer	
Bill Sisson	

After You Listen

Write a follow-up question you would like to ask one of the speakers, and identify to whom it would be directed.

_____

_____

Working in a group, ask and answer each other's follow-up questions. When a group member answers your question, try to think of another follow-up question to extend the discussion.

Academic
Survival Skill

Interpreting Charts

Charts can help an audience visualize an otherwise obscure list of facts and numbers. But even charts can overwhelm an audience if the speaker doesn't take time to clearly point out and explain the key features.

A. Read the following excerpt from Listening 1 and underline the sections where Tim Dixon refers to lines on the graph on page 70.

> "So between now and 2050, the world's urban population is expected to grow by something like 84 percent, or 6.3 billion people. Now that growth, as you can see from this graph, is concentrated primarily in the urban areas of the less developed regions where we're going to see something like an increase from 2.5 billion today, as represented by the vertical line, the dotted line there on the graph, to something like 5.2 billion in 2050. So there's a substantial growth of population. And this probably doesn't come as any surprise to people in the room. But the developed regions will grow less slowly in the world: the population there in 2050 in those regions is likely to be something like 1.2 billion compared with under a billion today; so a much slower growth trajectory as represented by the orange line on the graph."

B. Look at the following chart that compares the impact of different building materials on the environment. What would you say to compare wood, steel and concrete design? Write three statements that explain different portions of the chart.

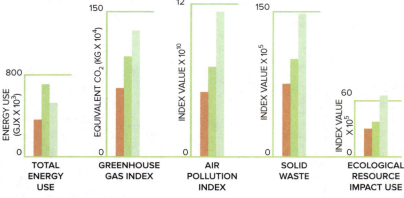

- Wood Design
- Steel Design
- Concrete Design

Source: Green by Design, Canadian Wood Council. (2004). Retrieved from http://www.cwc.ca/images/media/Green_By_Design.pdf

❶ _____

_____

_____

❷ _____

_____

_____

❸ _____

_____

_____

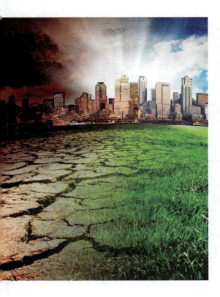

FINAL ASSIGNMENT
Participate in a Panel Discussion

Now it's your turn. Use everything you have learned in this chapter to prepare for and participate in a panel discussion.

A. Form groups of five and choose a topic related to sustainability and your community. For example, you might choose urban agriculture, public transportation or the conversion of a derelict building into a community space. Examine your topic in terms of the sustainable policies and practices in place now, if any, and the policies and practices to be put in place to promote sustainability. Because you're working in a group, generate a few topics and then choose one by consensus. Write a topic title at the top of the next page.

TOPIC: _____

B. Speak with your teacher. Ask for approval of your topic and advice on how to develop it.

C. Select a moderator, whose job it will be to introduce the topic as well as the members of the panel. The moderator's job also includes helping to elicit, rephrase and direct audience questions to the right panel member.

D. Meet as a group to organize the research and plan the panel discussion. Assign each member a different area of research. Have each find out as much as possible about the topic from different points of view. Observe practices, conduct interviews and do research.

> **OBSERVE:** Visit relevant locations and observe the sustainable practices in place to determine possible improvements that could be introduced. For example, a local daycare might have an organic garden with rainwater collection and recycling bins. What else could be done?

> **INTERVIEW:** If appropriate, explain your task to someone who has expert knowledge on your topic and request an interview. Ask basic questions and use follow-up questions to elicit other details. (See the different types of questions in the Focus on Speaking on page 56.)

> **RESEARCH:** Ask a librarian where you can find information about your topic as well as about sustainability practices in general. See what is available online. Some organizations, like community gardens, may offer online documentation and policies on sustainability. If you are suggesting a new initiative, such as establishing a network of bicycle lanes, review successful models from other cities. Keep complete records of each source, following the citation style preferred in your field of study.

E. Plan your panel discussion. Once each group member has collected information, meet again and, using the structure of the table on the next page, organize the group's ideas. If possible, have each speaker present a chart to help explain the issues. Structure the group's ideas around the key points that each designated speaker will present, with explanations and examples.

TOPIC: _____

SPEAKER 1 _____

AREA OF RESEARCH _____

- POINT 1 _____
  _____

- POINT 2 _____
  _____

- POINT 3 _____
  _____

SPEAKER 2 _____

AREA OF RESEARCH _____

- POINT 1 _____
  _____

- POINT 2 _____
  _____

- POINT 3 _____
  _____

MODERATOR
_____

SPEAKER 3 _____

AREA OF RESEARCH _____

- POINT 1 _____
  _____

- POINT 2 _____
  _____

- POINT 3 _____
  _____

SPEAKER 4 _____

AREA OF RESEARCH _____

- POINT 1 _____
  _____

- POINT 2 _____
  _____

- POINT 3 _____
  _____

F. Practise your panel discussion with your moderator, taking into account the above points and all your research.

G. Present your panel discussion in front of the class. After, meet to reflect on what went well and what could have gone better.

"We have an economy that tells us it is cheaper to destroy Earth in real time rather than renew, restore and sustain it. You can print money to bail out a bank but you can't print life to bail out a planet."
—Paul Hawken, environmentalist, entrepreneur and author (1946–)

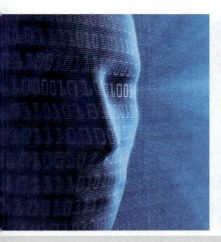

CRITICAL CONNECTIONS

Chapters 3 and 4 both dealt with technological (and other) enhancements—in the first case, to improve the human body, and in the second case, to improve cities. Now, you have the opportunity to put together everything you've learned and think critically to complete integrated tasks.

1 Augmented reality refers to the integration of computer-generated information into one's real-world environment. Typically, a mobile phone application uses GPS location and photo recognition software to map text and images onto a streetscape, visible through the phone's camera display. The information might include the names of places, historical details or current news. In the future, it's likely that special eyeglasses will integrate such technology. When and where would you want to wear them? Discuss in a group.

2 Consider the following quotation.

> "We are all physically disabled at some time in our lives. A child, a person with a broken leg, a parent with a pram, an elderly person, etc., are all disabled in one way or another ... As far as the built-up environment is concerned, it is important that it should be barrier-free and adapted to fulfill the needs of all people equally. As a matter of fact, the needs of the disabled coincide with the needs of the majority, and all people are at ease with them." (United Nations, 2003–04)

a) Working in a group, discuss the quotation. Then, research a building or urban area you know and consider ways in which it could be modified to meet the expectations expressed in the quotation. Address mobility, vision and hearing challenges. How could the building or area be further improved to appeal to individuals with an enhanced ability, such as enhanced vision or enhanced hearing?

b) Create a Likert scale questionnaire (see the Academic Survival Skill on page 61) and collect attitudes and opinions about your ideas for modifying your chosen building or area.

c) Divide responsibilities among your group members and share your findings and ideas with the class in a ten-minute presentation. Consider bar graphs to illustrate your survey results and a computer presentation with images of the building or area you propose to redesign.

Reference

United Nations. (2003–04). Accessibility for the disabled: A design manual for a barrier free environment. Retrieved from http://www.un.org/esa/socdev/enable/designm/intro.htm

COMPANION **web+** Visit the Companion Website for new content related to Chapters 3 and 4.

CHAPTER 5

Rise of the Citizen Journalist

Krakatoa's volcanic eruption on August 27, 1883 caused widespread devastation, killing at least 36,000 people. Because of the telegraph, the eruption was one of the first major events reported around the world within hours of its occurrence.

Social media technologies have extended the delivery of news through the contributions of "citizen reporters." Now, ordinary people, in extraordinary situations, instantly share news in text, photos and videos just seconds after a newsworthy event occurs. Others follow up with comments and opinions. The resulting news is not always perfectly accurate, but it features more detail and immediacy than the world has ever seen.

In this chapter, you will

- listen to lectures and an interview on the role of new media in journalism;
- learn vocabulary related to newsgathering and news sharing;
- learn to recognize repair, qualification and elaboration techniques;
- organize a news story using the inverted pyramid format;
- explain new ideas through comparisons;
- practise speaking individually, in pairs and in groups;
- prepare a podcast and take part in an interview.

GEARING UP

A. Consider the following diagram. Then, answer the questions that follow. Check with a classmate if you're uncertain of any of the social media terms.

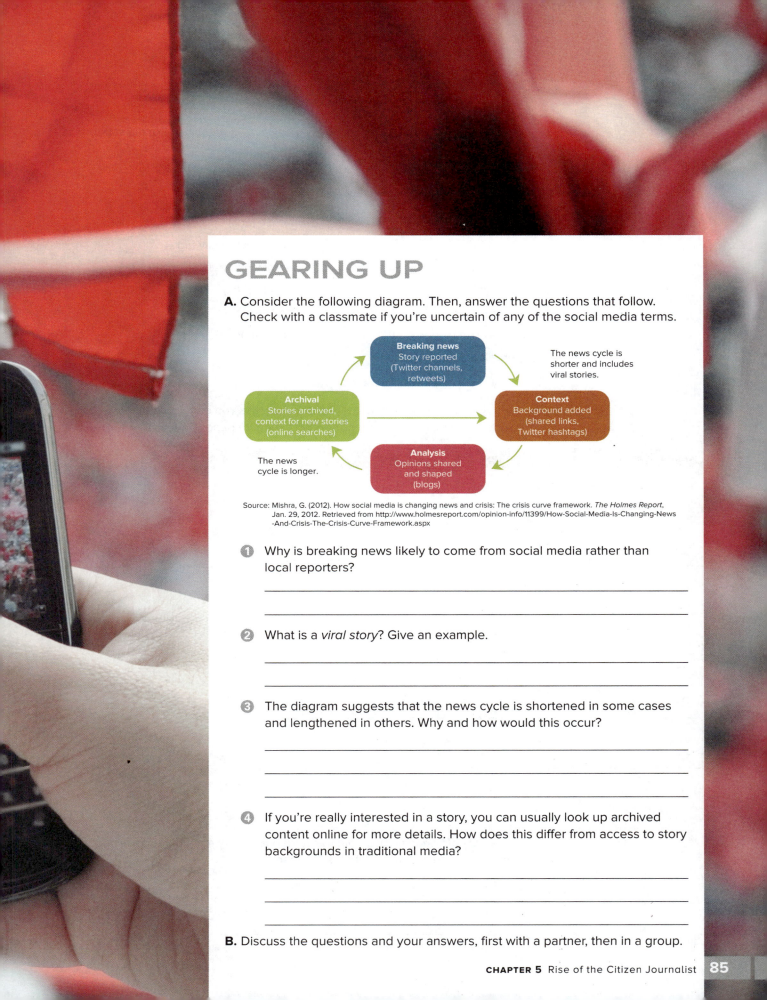

Breaking news
Story reported
(Twitter channels,
retweets)

The news cycle is
shorter and includes
viral stories.

Archival
Stories archived,
context for new stories
(online searches)

Context
Background added
(shared links,
Twitter hashtags)

The news
cycle is longer.

Analysis
Opinions shared
and shaped
(blogs)

Source: Mishra, G. (2012). How social media is changing news and crisis: The crisis curve framework. *The Holmes Report*, Jan. 29, 2012. Retrieved from http://www.holmesreport.com/opinion-info/11399/How-Social-Media-Is-Changing-News-And-Crisis-The-Crisis-Curve-Framework.aspx

1 Why is breaking news likely to come from social media rather than local reporters?

_____

_____

2 What is a *viral story*? Give an example.

_____

_____

3 The diagram suggests that the news cycle is shortened in some cases and lengthened in others. Why and how would this occur?

_____

_____

_____

4 If you're really interested in a story, you can usually look up archived content online for more details. How does this differ from access to story backgrounds in traditional media?

_____

_____

_____

B. Discuss the questions and your answers, first with a partner, then in a group.

A. Below are key words and phrases you will hear in Listening 1. Check the words you understand. Then, check the words you use.

	UNDERSTAND	USE		UNDERSTAND	USE
agitated (adj.)	☐	☐	politicking (n.)	☐	☐
bristled (v.)	☐	☐	power base (n.)	☐	☐
campaign (n.)	☐	☐	power brokers (n.)	☐	☐
capacity* (n.)	☐	☐	prolific (adj.)	☐	☐
cohort (n.)	☐	☐	pseudonymously (adv.)	☐	☐
curating (v.)	☐	☐	re-entrenchment (n.)	☐	☐
guise (n.)	☐	☐	scenario* (n.)	☐	☐
incarnation (n.)	☐	☐	scrutiny (n.)	☐	☐
incursion (n.)	☐	☐	tenets (n.)	☐	☐
perpetual (adj.)	☐	☐	unduly (adv.)	☐	☐

*Appears on the Academic Word List

B. Write a definition for each of the words or phrases you do not understand, using a dictionary and continuing on a separate sheet of paper if necessary.

WORD/PHRASE	DEFINITION

C. The word *politicking* comes from the word *politic*. Use each of the following words in a sentence that illustrates its meaning.

❶ politic (adj.): _____

_____

_____

② politics (n.): _____

_____

_____

③ political (adj.): _____

_____

_____

④ politically (adv.): _____

_____

_____

⑤ politician (n.): _____

_____

_____

D. The words and phrases in task A were taken from Listening 1, a lecture about social media journalism; however, several of these words are also used in politics. Write a paragraph describing a local, national or international political event. Use five words or phrases from task A.

_____

_____

_____

_____

_____

_____

_____

_____

_____

E. Working in a small group, read your paragraphs and discuss how social media might affect the reporting of political events.

FOCUS ON LISTENING

Listening for Repair, Qualification and Elaboration

When speakers are in conversation, or are giving presentations without strictly reading their notes, they are likely to use techniques called *repair*, *qualification* and *elaboration*. Repair is a correction: a speaker goes back to an earlier point to repeat a sentence or phrase, adjusting the information. A qualification is a statement that explains one or more exceptions to what has just been said. An elaboration adds information, to make a speaker's message clearer. Very often, these techniques are prefaced with a phrase that signals the type of correction that will be made.

A. Read the following examples of phrases that can be used with repair, qualification and elaboration techniques and add examples of your own. Compare your examples with those of a partner.

TECHNIQUE	EXAMPLE PHRASE	YOUR PHRASE
REPAIR	I mean, …	
QUALIFICATION	except for …	
ELABORATION	for example, …	

B. In the following excerpt from Listening 1, note how the speaker, Julie Posetti, uses questions in addition to repair, qualification and elaboration techniques to add content and effect to her presentation.

Posetti had already made a statement about making journalism social. She repeats it as a question to provide an opportunity for elaboration.

Posetti repairs her error of forgetting the "of" by backing up, adding "of" and repeating "journalism."

With "and is being done," Posetti elaborates, adding emphasis and immediacy to her statement.

Posetti puts into words what might be the audience's unspoken question, "What role can Twitter play?" thus providing another opportunity for elaboration.

> "So <u>what do I mean by making journalism social?</u>
>
> "Well, it's a story about the transformation jour-nalism, <u>of journalism, or at least some pockets of it</u>, into a truly community-engaged, interactive, collaborative process.
>
> "And I keep hearing journalists and other researchers say things like, 'Twitter isn't jour-nalism.' So, let's just get that out of the road upfront. <u>Of course Twitter isn't journalism; Twitter is a platform on which journalism can be done</u>—<u>and is being done</u>—minute by minute, second by second, in fact, around the world.
>
> "<u>And if you're in any doubt about the sort of role that a platform like Twitter can play—par-ticularly in a breaking news story</u>—just cast your mind back from the Osama bin Laden assas-sination, which was unwittingly live-tweeted by an Abbottabad computer programmer running a coffee shop."

Posetti answers her own question, but with a qualifying phrase, "or at least some pockets of it."

Posetti agrees but then qualifies the comment by repeating "Twitter" with a new definition.

Posetti's use of "particu-larly in a breaking news story" is another example of elaboration.

C. Rewrite the excerpt of Posetti's speech from task B, leaving out the questions and the repetitive aspects of repair, qualification and elaboration.

_____

_____

_____

_____

_____

_____

D. With your partner, compare your rewrites in task C to the original speech. Discuss how the use of questions, repair, qualification and elaboration clarifies information and adds effect to Posetti's speech.

Making Journalism Social: Twitter's Transformative Effect

Twitter, an online social networking and messaging service, is changing the way journalism is practised. Because it allows for only concise messages—140 characters in length, at most—posting on Twitter is considered "micro-blogging": the sharing of briefly stated ideas, news, opinions and questions. It allows users to capture and pass on information, often through the use of hashtags (# plus a key word) that identify the discussion thread. Julie Posetti, an Australian journalist and an academic at the University of Canberra, suggests that Twitter has the power to transform journalism by turning anyone with an account into a citizen reporter.

Before You Listen

In her lecture, Posetti uses several journalism terms that might be unfamiliar to many listeners: the term *masthead* refers to a newspaper or other publication, such as the *New York Times*, and a *tag line* is a branding slogan, such as that newspaper's "All the news that's fit to print." Posetti also mentions Chatham House Rules, which is actually only one rule. According to the Chatham House website:

> When a meeting, or part thereof, is held under the Chatham House Rule, participants are free to use the information received, but neither the identity nor the affiliation of the speaker(s), nor that of any other participant, may be revealed.

Why do you think the Chatham House Rule is used? Can you think of situations in which it would be either useful or problematic? Discuss your answers in a group.

_____

_____

_____

_____

_____

_____

_____

_____

How might the rise of social media journalism change the scope and application of the rule? Discuss your thoughts with your group.

In the following excerpt from Listening 1, Posetti discusses the news event that she feels demonstrated Twitter's first big impact on journalism: the 2009 Hudson River plane crash that involved the emergency landing of a plane on water after Canada geese struck and disabled its engines. All 155 passengers and crew were successfully evacuated from the sinking plane.

> "Right back to the first breaking news event that is associated with Twitter's incursion into daily journalism, which was the Hudson River plane crash. And that involved a ferry operator—or passenger, rather—on a ferry. The operator was taking the ferry to the rescue scene on the Hudson River. And he took a snap on his mobile phone of the plane crashed into the river, which you could recognize if you saw it, and that became viral almost instantly as a result of him posting it on Twitter, via his mobile phone, and it was shared around the world."

What would have made this incident so newsworthy? Discuss your answer with a partner.

_____

_____

_____

_____

While You Listen

The first time you listen, try to get the general idea. Listen a second time to take notes on each segment. Focus on the main message and consider whether the explanations and examples support the speaker's main ideas. Listen a third time to check your notes and add details.

SEGMENT	NOTES
I am also saying that this is a process of making journalism and journalists social because there's been quite a degree of resistance …	
So, it's not just a case of sitting in a newsroom and discussing what event you were just at and how you might report it and who else you might speak to.	
So, yeah—so, I mean literally, while some journalists early on got involved in social media through involvement particularly with Twitter, there are very many others who have refused to engage in the process of social journalism.	
So, while we've traditionally had involvement with audiences through interactions such as writing letters to the editor and through talkback radio, for example—which I originally cast as the first incarnation of social media—those were mediated platforms …	

SEGMENT	NOTES
And what's changed with social media is that, that traditional power base of journalists disseminating information from the top down and sitting from that position of power, determining how stories will be framed and how they should be interpreted, perhaps.	
So, journalism has always been about social engagement in the sense that journalists have sought information; they have asked questions; they have also desired to start a conversation.	
So, we've had a phase now of what people are calling "Journalism 1.0," if you like, which involved this engagement that I'm talking about based on an unequal power relationship ...	
So, what this means is that journalists had become not just people who were contributing ideas that should be debated but that they were also trying to ... elicit responses from audiences.	
And as a result of that re-entrenchment, the public became—instead of being enthusiastic about the role that journalists were playing through social media as they initially were ... they became increasingly agitated.	
And then we saw a process in the Australian setting of the other group of journalists, the journalists who were willing to engage and interact and incorporate the contributions of the community in the reframing of what it means to be a journalist and what journalism is ...	
The problem arises when in a situation like journalism as it currently stands, which is in a state of perpetual transformation ...	

After You Listen

Posetti's title for her lecture is "Making Journalism Social: Twitter's Transformative Effect." Based on your notes, how has Twitter already transformed journalism and what still needs to be transformed? Discuss your answer with a partner.

_____

_____

_____

_____

_____

_____

A. Below are key words and phrases you will hear in Listening 2 or Listening 3. Check the words you understand. Then, check the words you use.

	UNDERSTAND	USE		UNDERSTAND	USE
aggregate* (v.)	☐	☐	monopolist (adj.)	☐	☐
anecdote (n.)	☐	☐	nostalgia (n.)	☐	☐
bane (n.)	☐	☐	orthodoxy (n.)	☐	☐
churnalism (n.)	☐	☐	pundit (n.)	☐	☐
circular debates* (n.)	☐	☐	refrain (n.)	☐	☐
exploited* (v.)	☐	☐	sound bites (n.)	☐	☐
geotagging (n.)	☐	☐	taken root (v.)	☐	☐
leap of faith (n.)	☐	☐	tap into (v.)	☐	☐
mindset (n.)	☐	☐	validation* (n.)	☐	☐
monetize (v.)	☐	☐	verification (n.)	☐	☐

*Appears on the Academic Word List

B. Write a definition for each of the words or phrases you do not understand, using a dictionary and continuing on a separate sheet of paper if necessary.

WORD/PHRASE	DEFINITION

C. *Churnalism, geotagging* and *sound bites* are all examples of media neologisms—words or expressions created, or borrowed, to describe new phenomena. Match each of the following neologisms to its meaning.

NEOLOGISMS	MEANING
❶ community building (v.)	*6* contribute to a blog or forum
❷ forum (n.)	*9* mark online content in order to make it searchable
❸ friend (n.)	*8* subscription service for blogs and other social media
❹ lurker (n.)	*5* audio or video broadcast that can be downloaded
❺ podcast (n.)	*7* autobiographical information provided to a website
❻ post (v.)	*3* contact on a social networking site
❼ profile (n.)	*2* discussion area on a website
❽ Really Simple Syndication (RSS) (n.)	*4* person who reads but doesn't contribute to forums
❾ tag (v.)	*1* recruiting participants with shared interests
❿ thread (n.)	*10* conversation subtopic posted to a forum

D. Complete the following paragraph with words or phrases from task A.

Some people continue to read newspapers in a spirit of warm _____ and consider online media the _____ of professional journalism. However, many newspapers are controlled by _____ owners who shape the _____ of the public by repeating the same _____ in multiple publications. Websites that _____ the news tend to provide a wider range of views. Moreover, websites that _____ citizen reporters' blogs and tweets are likely to offer the widest range of views, even though opinions can be quite volatile. Because viewership for these websites might then increase, this inclusion of citizen reporters' opinions is _____ by some media outlets and companies that plant stories and _____ to be picked up and repeated by bloggers.

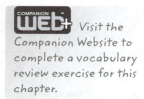
E. Discuss the paragraph in task D with a partner. Do you both agree with the ideas in the paragraph? Other than to reach a wider audience, why might a company plant stories on a blogger's website?

_____

_____

_____

LISTENING ② Breaking News: The Changing Relationship between Blogs and Mainstream Media

> People who naturally use Internet resources are called "digital natives."

How do you get your news? Do you listen to the radio, watch TV, read newspapers or go online? People increasingly find the latest information online, but not always from traditional news providers. If you use services such as Facebook and Twitter, you probably hear about current events not through a news website but through alerts from friends who have already seen, heard or read about what has happened. Richard Sambrook is a professor of journalism and director of the Centre for Journalism at Cardiff School of Journalism, Media and Cultural Studies. He thinks that new journalism, based on gathering and sharing information from social media sources, is disrupting the traditional model of journalism.

Before You Listen

Read the following excerpt from Listening 2 and consider possible short-term and long-term impacts of social media on traditional news media.

> "So, how does social media and traditional news media interact and what's been the impact of the one upon the other? And I suppose my headline, being a newsperson, would be that familiar refrain that I think the impact is overestimated in the short term and underestimated in the long term. And in relation to that, I think a lot of news organizations currently—certainly including the BBC—are going through great turmoil and disruption and struggling with that."

SHORT-TERM IMPACTS: _____

_____

_____

LONG-TERM IMPACTS: _____

_____

_____

While You Listen

The first time you listen, try to get the general idea. Listen a second time and take notes on each sound bite or concept and consider how each is defined or expanded upon. Listen a third time to check your notes and add details.

SOUND BITE / CONCEPT	NOTES
SOUND BITE 1: "We don't own the news any more."	
CITIZEN JOURNALISM	
ONLINE DISCUSSION (BLOGS AND TWITTER)	
PROGRAM: *World Have Your Say*	
TWITTER CORRESPONDENT	
SCIENCE JOURNALISM	
CONSTRUCT: NETWORK JOURNALISM	
SOUND BITE 2: "Transparency is the new objectivity."	
CULTURAL SHIFT	
SOUND BITE 3: "Information is not journalism."	

SOUND BITE / CONCEPT	NOTES
VOLATILITY (VOLATILE PERIOD)	
SOUND BITE 4: "If you find yourself in competition with the Internet, find a way out."	
FAITH IN PROFESSIONAL JOURNALISM	
FUNDAMENTAL SHIFT IN NEWSGATHERING	

After You Listen

Sambrook is concerned with the economic model for online media—getting users to pay for access to the news. Many online versions of newspapers and news magazines have tried to create subscription models in which users pay a monthly or annual fee. However, the widespread availability of alternative free sources means that few fee-charging services have been successful.

Answer the following questions. Then, discuss your answers in a group.

• What improved services would make you willing to pay for access to online news?

_____

_____

• Money from advertising subsidizes many online news sites. Would you be willing to pay for access to online news with no advertising? Explain your answer.

_____

_____

• Companies such as Facebook and Google already collect data on users and sell it to marketing companies. Would you be willing to provide more information about yourself in exchange for better online news services? Explain your answer.

_____

_____

Academic
Survival Skill

Organizing a News Story Using the Inverted Pyramid Format

Different kinds of information are shared in different ways. For example, a scientific report may begin with a summary and slowly lead the listener or reader through the steps of an investigation to a final conclusion. However, a news report often begins by presenting the key information, or conclusion, first and then the less important information and background details. This format allows a listener or reader to get the gist of a story and then decide whether or not the story is important or interesting enough to them to learn further details.

To deal with tight deadlines and limited space or time, news editors might cut an inverted pyramid story from the bottom if the extra information doesn't fit on the page or into the time slot.

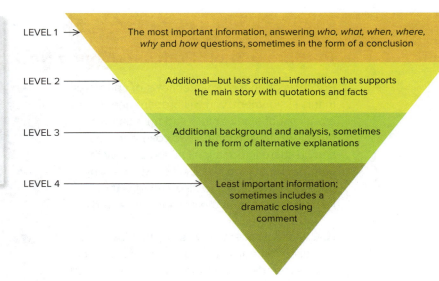

LEVEL 1 → The most important information, answering *who, what, when, where, why* and *how* questions, sometimes in the form of a conclusion

LEVEL 2 → Additional—but less critical—information that supports the main story with quotations and facts

LEVEL 3 → Additional background and analysis, sometimes in the form of alternative explanations

LEVEL 4 → Least important information; sometimes includes a dramatic closing comment

In online media, this model has changed slightly because extensive information can be added in the form of clickable links to other Web pages. Also, comments from readers or listeners can be added, and these may be as long as, or longer, than the original story.

A. Read the details of the following news story. For each section, consider the type of information presented and indicate its corresponding level—1, 2, 3 or 4—in an inverted pyramid format. Then, discuss your answers with a partner.

May 18, 2012—Facebook is listed on NASDAQ at $38 per share

Zuckerberg is married to Priscilla Chan, a physician. The pair met as students at Harvard University. LEVEL __4__

By listing Facebook on the NASDAQ, Zuckerberg's own shares put his net worth at US $9.8 billion. LEVEL __2__

Facebook had announced it would offer shares in February. LEVEL __3__

Facebook offered 421,233,615 shares of its common stock, which will trade on the NASDAQ under the symbol FB. LEVEL __2,3__

Facebook, the social network site, began publicly trading stock today. LEVEL __1__

Zuckerberg explained the shares would reward those who invested in and helped engineer Facebook. He said, "One of the ways you do that is to compensate people with equity and options." LEVEL __3__

Zuckerberg updated his Facebook status to indicate that he "listed a company on NASDAQ." LEVEL __4__

B. What other information would you want to know in order to better understand this news article? Discuss your answer with a partner.

_____

_____

_____

WARM-UP ASSIGNMENT
Prepare a Short Podcast about a News Event

Podcasts often feature interviews or speeches. In this assignment, you will prepare and record a podcast of a news story and then answer questions on it. In your news coverage, you should share information in a logical way that answers basic *who, what, when, where, why* and *how* questions and also engages the listener to reflect on the content presented.

A. Choose a recent news story that involved citizen journalism; ensure part of the story was reported by non-journalists using social media such as Twitter, Facebook or personal blogs. Speak with your teacher and ask for approval of your choice. The story should also include feedback and comments from the public. Look for information on your story from more than one source. Keep complete records of each source, following the citation and referencing guidelines of your discipline.

COMPANION **web+** *Visit the Companion Website to learn more about common citation and referencing guidelines.*

B. Use the inverted pyramid structure to organize your notes. Think of a dramatic final statement to inspire audience comments and questions.

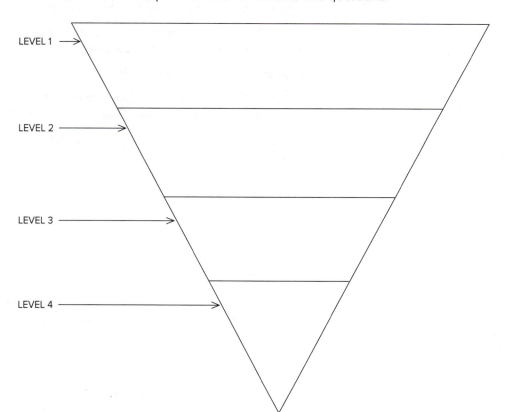

LEVEL 1

LEVEL 2

LEVEL 3

LEVEL 4

C. Now, use your notes to write out the full story, adding supporting details to prepare a five-minute script.

D. Practise your script with a partner, discussing how you can improve the content and delivery of your news story. When you are ready, record your podcast.

E. Play your recording to a small group of classmates. Be prepared to answer questions about your news story afterwards. Keep a record of any questions and comments that could improve your presentation; this will help you prepare for the Final Assignment.

FOCUS ON SPEAKING

Explaining through Comparisons

When introducing new ideas to an audience, it's helpful to relate them to something the audience is already familiar with. You can explain ideas in terms of similes and metaphors, making comparisons to show similarities. You can also refer to examples from the past to illustrate not just what is similar but also what has changed.

A. Read the following excerpts from Listening 2 and consider how Richard Sambrook examines and makes comparisons with the past to explain the role of new media in journalism.

FAMILIAR IDEAS

Sambrook relates using citizen journalists to the traditional practice of using eyewitnesses.

Sambrook suggests that radio phone-ins are a unique way of involving the audience.

Sambrook explains and criticizes the old model, in which journalists were sent abroad to cover stories.

❗ *Synchronous communication, such as chat, occurs in real time; asynchronous communication, such as e-mail, occurs at different times.*

"I mean, they've always used—they've always interviewed eyewitnesses, they've always used material from the public."

"You've had radio phone-ins, which have been a way of absorbing the opinions of the audience into programming and so on, giving access to the audience to programming—you've had that as a format for decades. I don't really yet see the kind of social media equivalent of that."

"So, you know, the old model, which has been decades old, that you have a bureau or you send someone from London or New York to go to a place that they don't know very well and talk to a few people and come back and tell you what they found—that's a model that, you know, I've grown up with and I've worked with, and though it's been great fun—but in a world of interconnection and in an ever-interdependent world with all kind of technology and the network capability we have, it increasingly feels like a really stupid way to do it."

DIFFERENCES

Sambrook's notion of continued use of material from the public ignores the public's role in distributing content.

Online comments can relate to evolving stories as updates occur and can also layer comments on other comments, adding this feedback asynchronously.

People still travel and comment on events in places that are not familiar to them, but local residents in these places add new perspectives.

B. How would you explain the following terms to someone who was not familiar with social media? Use comparisons to common things or events. Once you have written your explanations, share them with a partner. Identify differences and discuss your answers until you agree on the best explanations.

BLOGGING: _____

_____

_____

PHOTO SHARING: _____

_____

_____

BOOKMARKING: _____

_____

_____

CROWDSOURCING: _____

_____

_____

LISTENING ❸   ## On the Future of Online Journalism

Newspapers were first published in the 1600s and the first radio and television news broadcasts aired in the early twentieth century. By comparison, social media is extremely young. Facebook began in 2004, YouTube in 2005 and Twitter in 2006. However, these recent services have radically changed the nature of newsgathering and news distribution, as well as how people engage with the news. In this listening, Jian Ghomeshi, a radio show host, interviews Emily Bell, director of the Tow Center for Digital Journalism and previously the director of digital content for Guardian News and Media. The interview is more of a discussion, with Ghomeshi contributing several points and ideas.

Before You Listen

This interview relies on the audience knowing certain terms, publications and institutions. Match each of the items to its description.

ITEM	DESCRIPTION
❶ *Wall Street Journal*	__2__ British financial newspaper
❷ *Financial Times*	__7__ journal of international affairs
❸ long form	__4__ leading British newspaper
❹ *Guardian*	__10__ popular American newspaper
❺ press release	__1__ American financial newspaper
❻ Columbia	__9__ National Public Radio
❼ *Foreign Policy* magazine	__6__ American university with a good journalism school
❽ BBC, CBC, Al Jazeera	__3__ extended news coverage and analysis
❾ NPR	__5__ short statement issued to the press and used as the basis of news stories
❿ *Daily News*	__8__ three television stations, based in Britain, Canada and Qatar, respectively

Bell compares the *Encyclopaedia Britannica* to *Wikipedia*, suggesting that the latter is more reliable because mistakes are quickly corrected and facts (such as changes to national leadership) are constantly updated; a print encyclopedia is limited in its possibility for correction. Consider the following comparisons from 2012 (when *Encyclopaedia Britannica* ceased publication) and discuss with a partner why *Wikipedia* has become one of the most popular websites in the world.

FEATURE	*ENCYCLOPAEDIA BRITANNICA*	*WIKIPEDIA*
FIRST PUBLISHED	1771	2001
CONTRIBUTORS	100 full-time editors and more than 4,000 contributors, including 110 Nobel Prize winners and 5 US presidents	751,426 unpaid contributors/editors
NUMBER OF ENTRIES	65,000	3,890,000
COST	US $1,395	Free

Source: Silverman, M. (2012). Encyclopedia Britannica vs. Wikipedia. *Mashable*. Retrieved from http://mashable.com/2012/03/16/encyclopedia-britannica-wikipedia-infographic/

While You Listen

The first time you listen, try to get the general idea. Listen a second time and take notes. Consider how Ghomeshi prompts Bell through new information, questions and comments. Listen a third time to add details.

QUESTIONS/COMMENTS	NOTES
Well, let's talk about other news organizations because most news organizations now have an online presence but with varying degrees of success, as you know. What, what are some of the biggest mistakes you see them make?	

QUESTIONS/COMMENTS	NOTES
But when you say "locking up some of the content," that you're talking about the practice of making some parts of the site stuff that you have to pay for … That's not necessarily nostalgia for the past, is it?	
On that note, the "of the moment," the speed … Oftentimes, by the time it's on at your 6 p.m. or 10 p.m. news, … you've been reading it on Twitter for twelve hours already, right?	
But what is the trade-off between the immediacy and what we've had? … If the medium is the message, are there any disadvantages you see in us consuming stories online in shorter form rather than in newspapers?	
Churnalism.	
As the mediums change—as the platforms, rather, change—does the journalism change? … the big news stories of 2011 … Egypt and Tunisia and Libya and their connection to the online world … How has that, in your view, affected the way those stories are covered in the West?	
But, but the flip side, I suppose, would say, "How do we know what can be trusted, especially if they're nameless or in some cases faceless? How do we ensure standards of truth are being met?"	
Let me go one step further … is the Western media unduly ignoring other underlying causes of disruption or revolution—say, poverty, disenfranchised youth—by making the story, "Look, they're all on Twitter now!"	
No, you're absolutely right, it's there, I get it, yeah. The resource. And changing.	
But it's also swamped in, and swallowed, in some cases, in opinion and commentary— everybody's an expert, right, in the new world … Looking ahead, do you think this tendency might swallow everything or do you still see a place for objective journalism online?	

After You Listen

Summarize the main ideas of the Bell interview and share them in conversation with a partner. Ask questions to clarify your partner's summary.

_____

_____

_____

_____

FINAL ASSIGNMENT
Take Part in an Interview

Now it's your turn. Use everything you have learned in this chapter to revise and share the content of your podcast, not as a recording, but as an interview of approximately fifteen minutes. In this assignment, you will take on two roles: an expert answering questions and a reporter-interviewer asking questions.

A. Revisit the news story you selected for the Warm-Up Assignment (page 98) and conduct additional research. Find out more details in response to the comments and questions you received from other students at the end of your podcast presentation.

B. Plan for your interview. On a separate sheet of paper, use the inverted pyramid format to organize your ideas, building on your notes from the Warm-Up Assignment with the new information you've gathered. In the role of expert, you will need to be able to discuss each of your points as thoroughly as possible when answering the interviewer's questions.

C. Share notes with a partner; as you will act as each other's interviewers, you need to use your partner's notes to prepare questions for him or her. In the role of reporter-interviewer, you need to be aggressive, politely interrupting your partner to ask probing questions to find out more details about important points before your partner moves on to the next point. Review some of the repair, clarification and elaboration phrases from Focus on Listening (page 87) to help phrase your interruptions.

D. Practise the interview with your partner, taking turns as interviewer and interviewee. Don't write a script for the class presentation; instead, use brief notes and keep the interview conversational, adding new information, questions and comments as seems natural. In your answers to the interview questions, be prepared to use repair, qualification and elaboration techniques and to explain your ideas through comparisons. (See the Focus on Speaking on page 99.)

E. Conduct your interview in front of the class. Then, answer any questions other students might have. After, meet to reflect on what went well and what could have gone better.

"Social media is about sociology and psychology more than technology."
—Brian Solis, business and technology author and speaker (1970–)

CHAPTER 6
The Science of Creativity

Most children sing, dance, draw, paint and have countless creative ideas and pursuits. Creativity expert Edward de Bono writes, "Creativity involves breaking out of established patterns in order to look at things in a different way." Young children do this naturally because they neither know nor care about traditional boundaries. However, as they grow older, they may find themselves more self-conscious about expressing creativity, particularly if their schooling focuses mainly on facts and the need to know "the right answer." Some experts have expressed concern about this stifling effect because creativity is increasingly recognized as an essential part of critical thinking and problem solving in academia and business.

In this chapter, you will

- listen to an excerpt from an audiobook and a lecture on creativity, and watch excerpts from a lecture on creative design;

- learn vocabulary related to studies of the brain and creativity;

- assess technical details and their meanings;

- learn how to use examples to clarify;

- identify problems and evaluate arguments;

- practise speaking individually, in pairs and in groups;

- describe an example of the creative process and take part in a creative consultation.

GEARING UP

A. Consider the diagram. Then, answer the questions that follow.

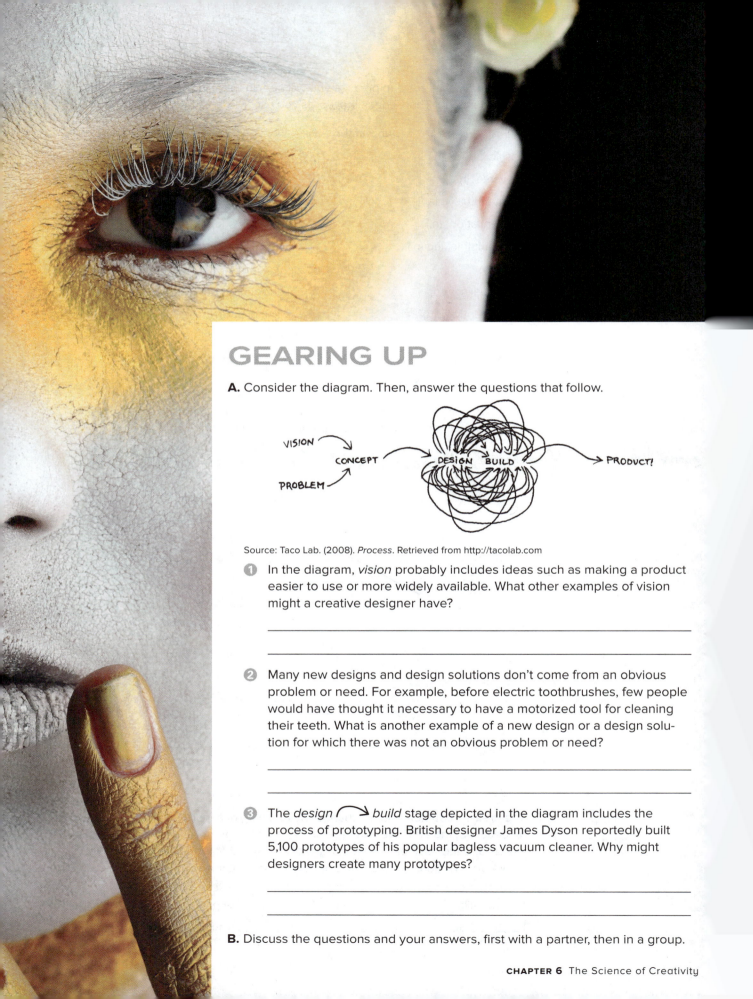

Source: Taco Lab. (2008). *Process*. Retrieved from http://tacolab.com

1 In the diagram, *vision* probably includes ideas such as making a product easier to use or more widely available. What other examples of vision might a creative designer have?

_____

_____

2 Many new designs and design solutions don't come from an obvious problem or need. For example, before electric toothbrushes, few people would have thought it necessary to have a motorized tool for cleaning their teeth. What is another example of a new design or a design solution for which there was not an obvious problem or need?

_____

_____

3 The *design* ⌢→ *build* stage depicted in the diagram includes the process of prototyping. British designer James Dyson reportedly built 5,100 prototypes of his popular bagless vacuum cleaner. Why might designers create many prototypes?

_____

_____

B. Discuss the questions and your answers, first with a partner, then in a group.

A. Below are key words and phrases you will hear in Listening 1. Check the words you understand. Then, check the words you use.

	UNDERSTAND	USE		UNDERSTAND	USE
classic model* (n.)	☐	☐	neural (adj.)	☐	☐
converse* (n.)	☐	☐	organizational life (n.)	☐	☐
counterintuitive (adj.)	☐	☐	rebranding (n.)	☐	☐
differentiation* (n.)	☐	☐	receptive (adj.)	☐	☐
dominant thinking (n.)	☐	☐	renowned (adj.)	☐	☐
EEG (n.)	☐	☐	reverie (n.)	☐	☐
freewheeling (adj.)	☐	☐	shooting it down (v.)	☐	☐
inadvertently (adv.)	☐	☐	sink or swim (v.)	☐	☐
integration* (n.)	☐	☐	spontaneous (adj.)	☐	☐
intently (adv.)	☐	☐	useful fiction (n.)	☐	☐

*Appears on the Academic Word List

B. Write a definition for each of the words or phrases you do not understand, using a dictionary and continuing on a separate sheet of paper if necessary.

WORD/PHRASE	DEFINITION

C. The prefixes *counter-* and *re-* change the meaning of a word by indicating, respectively, the opposite and repetition. Add *counter-* or *re-* to the following words, and then use each new word in a sentence that illustrates its meaning. Check your dictionary to see whether the words you form require hyphens.

_____ align		_____ create		_____ interpret		_____ productive
_____ argument		_____ culture		_____ invent		_____ proposal

1 _____

_____

2 _____

_____

3 _____

_____

4 _____

_____

5 _____

_____

6 _____

_____

7 _____

_____

8 _____

_____

D. Write a paragraph about a real-world problem for which a creative solution was found. Use at least five words or phrases from task A.

_____

_____

_____

_____

_____

_____

_____

_____

_____

_____

E. Working in a small group, read and discuss your paragraphs. Compare examples and look for common ideas about creative problem solving.

FOCUS ON LISTENING

Assessing Technical Details

Speakers sometimes mention technical details that their audiences are unlikely to understand. In some cases, speakers forget—or have not taken the time to learn—their audiences' level of technical expertise. In other cases, technical details are added simply to give the appearance of expertise. The technical details included may or may not be followed by explanations. When listening, it's important to link terminology to explanations and, at the same time, to think of other, more memorable ways to recall the information.

A. Read the following excerpt from Listening 1 without reading the explanatory notes in blue. Then, read the notes and relate them to the underlined terms. How much of the excerpt did you understand without reading the explanations?

An "Aha!" moment is defined as a sudden insight.

Gamma activity is a type of electrical brain activity occurring at frequencies between 25 and 100 Hz. A gamma spike is a moment of high activity.

A neural network is the set of pathways that allow specific neurons to interconnect.

The neocortex is the top layer of the brain in mammals and is the area responsible for higher brain functions, such as spatial reasoning.

"Brain studies on creativity reveal what goes on at that 'Aha!' moment, when we get a sudden insight. If you measure EEG brainwaves during a creative moment, it turns out there is very high gamma activity that spikes 300 milliseconds before the answer comes to us. Gamma activity indicates the binding together of neurons, as far-flung brain cells connect in a new neural network—as when a new association emerges. Immediately after that gamma spike, the new idea enters our consciousness.

"This heightened activity focuses on the temporal area, a centre on the side of the right neocortex. This is the same brain area that interprets metaphor and 'gets' jokes. It understands the language of the unconscious, what Freud called the 'primary process': the language of poems, of art, of myth. It's the logic of dreams, where anything goes and the impossible is possible."

Listeners are unlikely to know the meaning of "EEG" (electroencephalogram), but here, the context gives a sense of its purpose.

A millisecond is 1/1000 of a second. Three hundred milliseconds could be expressed as roughly a third of a second.

Neurons are cells that process and share information electrically and chemically. "Farflung brain cells" doesn't define neurons.

The temporal areas, on each side of the brain, process information from the senses and hold visual memories and emotions.

B. Using what you understand of the excerpt and the notes, write a summary, avoiding as much of the technical language as possible.

_____

_____

_____

_____

_____

_____

_____

_____

C. Almost everyone is an expert on something. Working with a partner, briefly explain a technical concept you understand well, deliberately using technical language. Then, have your partner summarize what you've said and say it back to you. How well was your partner able to understand your explanation? How well were you able to understand your partner's? Discuss what was easy and what was difficult in the exchange of information.

The Creative Brain

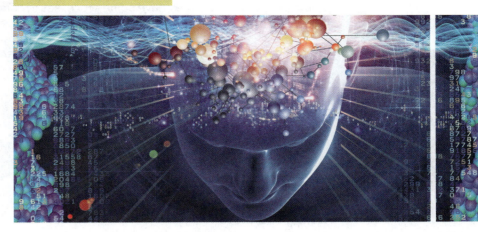

Scientists have long wondered whether the brain of a highly creative person is special in some way. One measure of a creative mind is the ability to engage in divergent thinking—intuitively considering several solutions to a problem. Divergent thinking is a technique of creative problem solving that can be taught. By measuring electrical activity in the brain of a person engaging in divergent thinking, the moment of a creative insight can be observed.

Daniel Goleman is an author, psychologist and science journalist best known for his work on emotional intelligence. In Listening 1, an excerpt from his audiobook *The Brain and Emotional Intelligence: New Insights*, Goleman describes the processes taking place in the brain when creative insights arise.

> ❗ *Emotional intelligence refers to the ability to understand and control one's emotions as well as those of others.*

Before You Listen

Goleman talks about several parts of the human brain. Consider the following diagrams and then try to link each of the given terms to its function.

left hemisphere
right hemisphere

temporal areas

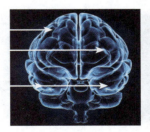

neocortex

amygdala
subcortical regions

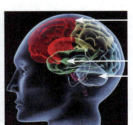

TERM	FUNCTION
❶ right hemisphere	_____ processes memory and emotions
❷ left hemisphere	_____ controls auditory functions
❸ amygdala	_____ controls the left half of the body
❹ subcortical regions	_____ controls cardiac and respiratory functions
❺ neocortex	_____ controls the right half of the body
❻ temporals areas	_____ processes language, learning, memory and complex thought

Working in a group, identify five creative people. What do you know about their creative processes? Do they have some processes in common? Write their names below and note whether their processes seem practical or impractical to you.

CREATIVE PEOPLE	PRACTICAL	IMPRACTICAL
_____	☐	☐
_____	☐	☐
_____	☐	☐
_____	☐	☐
_____	☐	☐

While You Listen

The first time you listen, try to get the general idea. Listen a second time and take notes on each segment. Focus on the main message and consider whether the explanations and examples support the speaker's main ideas. Listen a third time to check your notes and add details.

SEGMENT	NOTES
Right hemisphere	
Left hemisphere	
Creative brain	
Classic model of the four stages of creativity	
EXAMPLE: George Lucas	
EXAMPLE: Phil Glass	
EXAMPLE: Adrienne Weiss	
Brain studies on creativity	
Temporal area, on the side of the right neocortex	

SEGMENT	NOTES
High gamma spike	
How to mobilize this brain activity to get to the next stage	
Moments of spontaneous creative insights	
Relevance of the three or four classical stages of creativity	
How to create the conditions for a gamma spike	
Fourth stage: implementation	

After You Listen

With a partner, discuss a recent insight or creative idea you had. Identify moments in your thought process leading to this idea and relate them to the four stages of creativity. When you and your partner have both completed this task, share your thoughts in a group.

VOCABULARY BUILD

A. Below are key words and phrases you will hear in Listening 2 or Listening 3. Check the words you understand. Then, check the words you use.

	UNDERSTAND	USE		UNDERSTAND	USE
assimilate (v.)	☐	☐	political correctness (n.)	☐	☐
divine intervention* (n.)	☐	☐	quick and dirty (adj.)	☐	☐
dyslexia (n.)	☐	☐	radical (adj.)	☐	☐
embedded (v.)	☐	☐	regurgitate (v.)	☐	☐
empathy (n.)	☐	☐	resonates (v.)	☐	☐
emulates (v.)	☐	☐	seats at the table (n.)	☐	☐
false humility (n.)	☐	☐	silos (n.)	☐	☐
ghettoizing (v.)	☐	☐	thought experiments (n.)	☐	☐
intellectual rigour (n.)	☐	☐	traction (n.)	☐	☐
non-linear (adj.)	☐	☐	ubiquitous (adj.)	☐	☐

*Appears on the Academic Word List

B. Write a definition for each of the words or phrases you do not understand, using a dictionary and continuing on a separate sheet of paper if necessary.

WORD/PHRASE	DEFINITION

C. The expressions *seats at the table* and *silos* are examples of nouns of place with figurative (creative) meanings in the academic or business worlds, which are different from their literal (exact) meanings. Write sentences for each of the following expressions, using their figurative meanings.

1 corner office: _____

_____

_____

2 fence-sitting: _____

_____

_____

3 fork in the road: _____

_____

_____

4 glass ceiling: _____

_____

_____

5 safe harbour: _____

_____

_____

6 under the table: _____

_____

_____

D. Listening 2 deals with creativity—and especially the lack of emphasis on creativity—in the school system. Using at least seven words or phrases from task A, write a paragraph outlining what schools could do to encourage and support creative thinking.

_____

_____

_____

_____

_____

_____

_____

_____

COMPANION WEB+ Visit the Companion Website to complete a vocabulary review exercise for this chapter.

E. Working in a small group, read and discuss your paragraphs. What ideas do you share? Which would be the easiest to put into practice and which would be the most difficult?

LISTENING ② Science and Creativity

Gerard Darby is a trainer and writer who has worked with the Royal Society for the encouragement of Arts, Manufactures and Commerce, better known as the RSA. The organization's slogan is "twenty-first-century enlightenment." The Enlightenment was a period in the seventeenth and eighteenth centuries when philosophical, scientific and social revolutions created a new world view aimed at improving life for everyone.

Before You Listen

Darby talks about offering creative-thinking workshops. Read the excerpt on the next page, which is an abridged version of the introduction of his speech. Check with a partner and then a dictionary if there are any words you don't understand.

"For many years, I've been running workshops on creative thinking. In these workshops, I get participants to consider problems which they have to develop imaginative solutions to … I try and get people on these workshops to be almost childlike in their thinking and tap into that suppressed part of themselves that wants to be playful, to imagine, to try things out and to experiment. My aim is not to help the participants to learn to be creative but rather to relearn it because creative thinking is an innate part of ourselves, which we can lose touch with or, much more common, have it squeezed out of us. And the biggest culprit of that is education."

Imagine a situation or activity that would force your classmates to think creatively in order to come up with more than one solution to a problem; for example, the most efficient way to stack the chairs and tables in the classroom so that they take up the smallest possible amount of space. Write down your situation or activity, and then describe it to the class. As a class, try the best one.

_____

_____

_____

_____

While You Listen

Read the topic sentences in the first column. Then, the first time you listen, try to get the general idea. Listen a second time and take notes on each segment. Listen a third time to check your notes and add details.

TOPIC SENTENCE	NOTES
Our schooling is all about being right.	
I give students on my workshops different puzzles to solve, with the aim of making them reflect on how they've approached the challenges and how they thought about them.	
The world that today's young people are growing up in is changing faster than ever before.	
On my creative thinking course, as well as championing mistakes, I endorse day-dreaming, I encourage students to seek answers from one another and, if necessary, to copy each other when they get stuck.	
When a student is daydreaming, he or she is processing information and then may assimilate this into ideas—and that's a good thing, isn't it?	

TOPIC SENTENCE	NOTES
When students with dyslexia and other special learning needs come into my classes, I'm particularly pleased.	
Whenever I talk to teachers about creativity, they automatically start talking about an arts-based subject.	
I'm actively involved in the RSA, whose impressive building this is being recorded in.	
Now science. How we overlook the contribution of creative thinking to scientific discovery, ...	
If you go back to your old school, you'll get an overwhelming sense of nostalgia.	
I was talking to a small digital agency ... and they've created four new positions ... jobs that never existed in the company before and ones that they did not even anticipate making, ...	
Teachers, in my opinion, are on the whole pretty creative.	
But I don't think you can teach creative thinking.	
Now don't get me wrong. There are some wonderful interventions happening in schools to broaden students' minds.	
The issue is that these sorts of initiatives are bolt-ons, occasional treats, largely marginal to how learning takes place when, in fact, they should be at the heart of it.	

After You Listen

Darby is highly critical of the experiences most students have in traditional school settings, citing the lack of opportunity for creative thinking. During your own secondary education, what classroom experience gave you the most opportunity to express yourself creatively? Write notes and then compare your experiences in a group.

_____

_____

_____

_____

_____

WARM-UP ASSIGNMENT
Describe an Example of the Creative Process

People often look at the results of the creative process and can't imagine how someone developed a new idea. But, as mentioned by Daniel Goleman in Listening 1, inventors and designers commonly follow four steps in their creative process, either consciously or unconsciously. These are often referred to as *preparation, incubation, illumination* and *implementation*. Preparation involves defining a problem or goal and then collecting background information. During incubation, the problem or goal and the information are examined from different perspectives. Illumination is the stage during which the mind works to find an innovative solution to the problem or innovative processes by which the goal can be reached. Finally, implementation involves testing and sharing the solution, sometimes creating multiple alternatives or prototypes in response to feedback.

WEB+ *Visit the Companion Website to learn more about common citation and referencing guidelines.*

A. Working with a partner, identify a creative use for something ordinary. Or, find a product, or part of a product, that has been made from materials recycled for use in a new way. For example, in the impoverished village of Cateura, Paraguay, a musical director began making traditional musical instruments for a teenagers' orchestra, using cast-off materials from a landfill. One instrument, a cello, was constructed from an oil can, carved bits of waste wood and discarded kitchen tools.

B. Do your research. Look for background on the creative solution that was found and, if possible, learn about the people who created the new product and about the process they went through. Keep complete records of each source.

C. Structure your presentation according to the four steps in the creative process. Take notes in the table on the next page. If you do not have information on one or more of the creative stages, speculate, adding your own ideas of likely thought processes and their application in this specific instance.

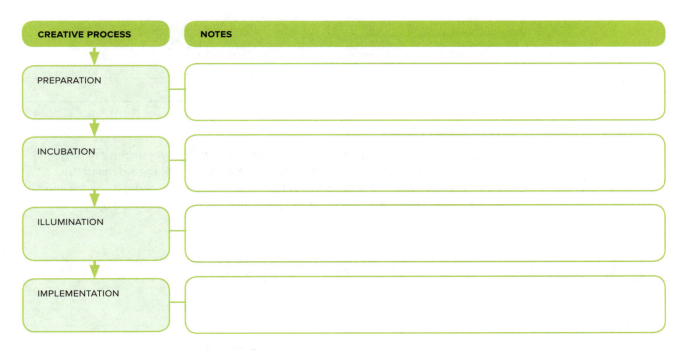

CREATIVE PROCESS	NOTES
PREPARATION	
INCUBATION	
ILLUMINATION	
IMPLEMENTATION	

D. Work with your partner to present your creative solution to the class, sharing the stages of its development that you noted in task C.

E. During your presentation, another pair of students will be asked to give feedback. One of the students will act as an "angel's advocate," as described in Listening 1, supporting and praising the creative process and solution described. The other student will act as a "devil's advocate," highlighting shortcomings in the process or solution by promoting a different viewpoint. Neither role depends on expressing personal ideas or feelings; in a business meeting, for example, angel's or devil's advocates may be called on to support or criticize an idea regardless of their opinion of it.

A "devil's advocate" helps avoid "group-think," in which everyone agrees with an idea, perhaps because a friend or person in charge has proposed it.

LISTENING ③

Creative Confidence: Cultivating the Mindset of Today's Innovators

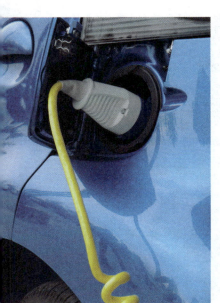

David Kelley, an entrepreneur, designer, engineer and teacher, is best known for his work with the design and innovation firm IDEO. Speaking at the Aspen Ideas Festival in 2011, he outlines the role of the designer in innovation processes, providing examples to clarify his points.

Before You Listen

Read Kelley's opening points.

> "Lots of interesting things have been happening in the design profession in recent years. And I thought maybe I'd share some of those with you. I think that the, the reason that design has become more prominent is because of our tie to innovation, that—designers have always been known as capable of painting a picture of a positive future with their ideas in it, right. And if you think about it, that's really what innovation is, is having those kind of breakthrough ideas about the future, right. And so, so we as designers are being called on to work on really very interesting projects in the innovation space. So it's been really exciting for us these last few years."

Kelley, speaking without notes, repeats himself. What are his main points?

_____

_____

_____

While You Listen

Read the following points and notes. Then, the first time you listen, try to get the general idea. Listen a second time and match each of the points in the first column to its note in the second column. The first one has been done for you as an example. Listen a third time to check your matches and to add details to complete the notes.

POINTS	NOTES
❶ Approach to innovation	_18_ solar lantern that … *replaces the need for kerosene*
❷ People say, "Oh, you're so creative."	_____ low-cost sleeping bag "incubator" developed for …
❸ Places like Stanford and at IDEO	_____ interactive reading experience …
❹ A mindset	_____ based on the diversity of …
❺ People who are natural design thinkers	_____ bias toward action and …
❻ Methodology called *design thinking*	_____ building empathy for …
❼ Human-centred design	_____ encouraged to argue points in front of a class because avoiding the notion of one "right" answer …
❽ "Keep the Change" for Bank of America	_____ everybody's creative, but …
❾ Culture of prototyping	_____ do everything …
❿ Sesame Street	_____ allowed fifty or one hundred thousand people to …

POINTS	NOTES
⑪ Pulse	_____ low-cost prototype video to find out ...
⑫ Storytelling	_____ helping people build ...
⑬ Alice	_____ how you innovate and where you get ...
⑭ Radical collaboration	_____ iPad news app ...
⑮ Stanford faculty	_____ way of thinking about the world and yourself; a bias toward ...
⑯ OpenIDEO	_____ savings plan based on ...
⑰ Embrace	_____ quick videos help users to ...
⑱ Delight	_____ looking at innovation as something you can do routinely; you have to be ...

After You Listen

At the end of Listening 3, Kelley says, "I don't care if the decisions are throwing a better dinner party or curing cancer, those are all important decisions ..." Is he right to make such comparisons? How does Kelley play devil's advocate in his own process of prototyping? Does learning about Kelley's perspectives on design make you more likely to examine the choices you make? Discuss your ideas with a partner and then in a group.

_____

_____

_____

_____

Clarifying with Examples

Examples in a speech illustrate abstract points in a concrete way. Rather than asking an audience to imagine how theoretical ideas might work, you can give them examples that help them understand how the theory is applied in real life.

A. Read the following excerpts from Listenings 1 and 3 to learn how examples can be used in a speech to enhance the audiences' understanding of it.

PURPOSE OF EXAMPLES	EXCERPTS
Examples are used both positively and negatively. A positively described example of an idea, such as the "Keep the Change" campaign, might be used in a persuasive speech.	DAVID KELLEY: "So we incorporated the kind of things we learned from them into a, in an offering called 'Keep the Change' ... So anyway, so, long story short, 2.5 million new customers in the first year, twelve million new customers—hard to get customers in a bank—and this is a wild success."
A discarded idea can be used as an example of how something imperfect can serve as a starting point for thinking of a better idea.	DK: "We sent them over to look at water, they went and looked at water, but one of the groups—one of the things about design is you're allowed to change the problem you're working on; you don't have to just do the problem that you were given. If you find a better problem, you work on that better problem. And they, when looking at water, noticed that kids were—their lungs were being filled with carbon from the kerosene in the lanterns in the little rooms, and they decided to take on that problem instead of water."
Examples can be presented by moving from the general to the specific—for example, by starting with a description of a problem and then proceeding to a specific example that addresses the problem. This technique is best used when the audience may not understand the situation.	DK: "Turns out there are millions of babies dying in India every year because of low birth weight, and they can't keep themselves warm ... And they [students] made this ... sleeping bag, right. It has paraffin wax that you can heat up in it ... and they believe hundreds of thousands of babies' lives will be saved ... From a company called Embrace. Started in one of our classes."
Specific examples can be described before explaining how they relate to larger issues—for example, by starting with the solution to a problem and then explaining why it was necessary.	DK: "Delight is a, is a solar lantern that replaces kerosene ... And they, when looking at water, noticed that kids were—their lungs were being filled with carbon from the kerosene in the lanterns in the little rooms, and they decided to take on that problem instead of water."
Examples of exceptions help deflect audience criticisms of the points presented.	DANIEL GOLEMAN: "This model is accurate to a point—but life is not that simple. I've found that people whose professions demand a stream of creative insights have a more complicated relationship to creativity than a neat four-stage model suggests. George Lucas, for example, ..."
A particularly powerful type of example is a personal story. Sharing a story about one's own experience gives the audience a sense of authenticity.	DAVID KELLEY: "But it's my point of view that at some point kids opt out of the, of being creative, you know. That for me, I wasn't that athletic, and so I said to everybody, 'I'm not good at sports,' right, or 'I'm not athletic.' "

B. Write specific examples that would further explain the ideas on the next page. Then, share your examples in a group.

1 a use of something for an unintended purpose: _____

_____

2 a show of empathy: _____

_____

3 a display of political correctness: _____

_____

4 a use of a product that led to horrible consequences: _____

_____

5 a useful fiction: _____

_____

C. Think of a problem you experienced and the creative solution you found to solve it. Describe the experience in three different ways, using different types of examples to help clarify.

THE PROBLEM AND THEN THE SOLUTION: _____

_____

_____

_____

THE SOLUTION AND THEN THE PROBLEM: _____

_____

_____

_____

BASED ON A TRUE STORY: _____

_____

_____

_____

D. Share your experience with a partner. Discuss the effectiveness of your examples.

Academic
Survival Skill

Identifying Problems and Evaluating Arguments

All organizations eventually face problems for which they require creative solutions. However, there is often a challenge in identifying the exact problem and then evaluating arguments in favour of implementing a particular solution.

A. In Listening 3, David Kelley mentions several creative solutions to problems in developing countries. Read the following paragraph and summarize the problem in your own words.

> "Studies in developing countries have shown that up to 20–25 percent of household food expenditure is incurred outside the home, and some segments of the population depend entirely on street foods … In many developing countries, street food vendors are an important component of the food supply chain … Food safety is a major concern with street foods. These foods are generally prepared and sold under unhygienic conditions, with limited access to safe water, sanitary services or garbage disposal facilities. Hence street foods pose a high risk of food poisoning due to microbial contamination, as well as improper use of food additives, adulteration and environmental contamination." (FAO/WHO, 2003)

_____

_____

_____

_____

_____

_____

_____

_____

B. A solution to a problem is usually achieved by addressing one or more factors of a situation. One factor mentioned in the above situation is the unhygienic conditions of street food preparation. Working in a group of six, form three teams of two. Each team will choose one of the following solutions and argue in favour of it while the rest of the group challenges the team's arguments. Using the table on the next page, note arguments both for and against each solution so that you will be prepared to participate in the group discussion.

- an information campaign to educate food vendors
- a community kitchen supervised by a health inspector
- an approval system using stickers to assure consumers of a food's quality

C. As a team, present your arguments for your chosen solution. Then, answer your group members' challenges as best you can.

D. When all three teams have presented their arguments and defended their chosen solution, as a group, propose one additional solution to the problem of unsafe street food. Note arguments for and against that solution, then compare it with the solutions in task B and rate all four in terms of likely effectiveness.

© **ERPI** • Reproduction prohibited

POSSIBLE SOLUTIONS	ARGUMENTS IN FAVOUR	ARGUMENTS AGAINST
• an information campaign to educate food vendors		
• a community kitchen supervised by a health inspector		
• an approval system using stickers to assure consumers of a food's quality		
•		

Reference

FAO/WHO. (2003). *Assuring food safety and quality: Guidelines for strengthening national food control systems*. Retrieved from http://www.fao.org/docrep/006/y8705e/y8705e06.htm

FINAL ASSIGNMENT
Take Part in a Creative Consultation

Now it's your turn. Use everything you have learned in this chapter to research and participate in a creative consultation of up to fifteen minutes.

A. Form a group of six, and decide on a situation where you can apply creative thinking to a real-world problem. The situation can be local, national or international, but it should be a complicated problem that invites divergent thinking and more than one solution.

CONSULTATION TOPIC: _____

B. Speak with your teacher. Ask for approval of the topic and advice on how to develop it.

C. Assign one of the following roles to each member of the group. The role will govern how he or she formulates solutions and reacts to ideas put forward in the consultation.

- a decision maker, who chairs the meeting, sets the agenda and time and calls on others to speak
- a dreamer, who asks hypothetical questions
- a realist, who considers costs and timelines
- an angel's advocate, who promotes new ideas
- a devil's advocate, who looks for shortcomings in new ideas
- a note taker, who separates and summarizes ideas and gives feedback throughout the consultation

These roles can overlap during the meeting, but agreeing ahead of time on each member's main responsibilities will ensure that all aspects of a good creative consultation are covered.

D. Do your individual research from the perspective of your assigned role, finding out as much as possible about the topic. Keep complete records of each source, following the citation and referencing guidelines of your discipline.

E. Conduct your consultation meeting in front of the class, sitting at a separate table and interacting only with the other members of your group. The note taker may want to take notes on the board, and the decision maker must ensure that everyone in the group has the opportunity to speak and to offer a perspective. At the end of your meeting, allow time for questions or comments from the class.

F. Listen as other groups conduct their meetings. As each group speaks, take notes and be prepared to ask questions.

G. Discuss the presentations as a class and evaluate those that were the most successful at suggesting solutions to real-world problems and those that could have been more effective.

"Imagination is not only the uniquely human capacity to envision that which is not, and therefore the fount of all invention and innovation. In its arguably most transformative and revelatory capacity, it is the power that enables us to empathize with humans whose experiences we have never shared."
—J.K. Rowling, author (1965–)

CRITICAL CONNECTIONS

In Chapter 5, you explored ideas about social media and citizen journalism. In Chapter 6, you focused on creativity, which is essential to problem solving. Now you have the opportunity to put together everything you've learned and think critically to complete integrated tasks.

1. Brevity is important in certain social media platforms. Twitter, for example, became popular by giving people the opportunity to micro-blog, sharing messages (including news reports and comments) of 140 characters or less. Read the following news item and summarize it in a message of up to 140 characters.

> "Because creative ideas are also new, they seem to give rise to uncertainty or even discomfort for others who depend on the tried-and-true way of doing things. To reduce uncertainty, subconsciously rejecting a creative idea may be easier than accepting it. Even in cases in which creative ideas show promise, it's still hard for other people to accept them, researchers say. Many people may not notice their inner bias against creativity and it may even get in the way of recognizing creative ideas, according to [a] study" (English, 2011).

2. Write a 140-character response to this news story, giving your perspective.

3. The short-messaging format of micro-blogging not only keeps communication concise, it also gives the reader more creative freedom to imagine the fuller story. In a group, discuss how this is likely to create a broader conversation, particularly when additional comments may be based more on opinion than on fact.

4. Micro-blogging has been used in attempts at new forms of creative writing, such as *twaiku*—haiku (a Japanese poetry form) for Twitter. Attempts at 140-character forms of fiction have also been made. For example, consider the following short story by British writer Ian Rankin, written in response to a Twitter fiction challenge in the *Guardian* newspaper:

> "I opened the door to our flat and you were standing there, cleaver raised. Somehow you'd found out about the photos. My jaw hit the floor."

In a group, discuss whether such short forms of literature are likely to become popular.

Reference

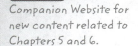 Visit the Companion Website for new content related to Chapters 5 and 6.

English, M. (2011, August 31). Creativity not as well received as we think. *Discovery News*. Retrieved from http://news.discovery.com/human/psychology/creativity-110831.htm

Body of Research

In the nineteenth century, a shortage of bodies for medical school anatomy classes meant that professors paid body snatchers to retrieve freshly buried bodies. Public outrage over the practice led to changes in the law, allowing for easier access to bodies if people chose to offer them freely. Today, many people donate their bodies to science, not only for dissection in the training of student doctors but also for transplants of various organs and for research in pathology—the study and diagnosis of disease.

Still, cultural, ethical, religious and even legal issues stop many people from donating their bodies or body parts after death, regardless of how useful such donations might be.

In this chapter, you will

- listen to interviews about stolen cells, contemporary dissections and historical pathology;

- learn vocabulary related to medicine, pathology and medical ethics;

- learn how to conduct interviews;

- explore the Harkness method for seminar discussion;

- focus on listening for paraphrase;

- practise speaking individually, in pairs and in groups;

- prepare and deliver one short presentation and take part in a seminar.

GEARING UP

A. Consider the chart. Then, answer the questions that follow.

Organ donor rates
Per million population, 2010

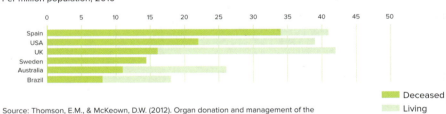

Source: Thomson, E.M., & McKeown, D.W. (2012). Organ donation and management of the
potential organ donor. *Anaesthesia & Intensive Care Medicine, 13*(6), 252–258.
Retrieved from http://www.sciencedirect.com/science/article/pii/S1472029912000744

1. Why might Spain have such a high rate of donation for deceased
   donors? Why might Brazil have such a low rate?

   _____

   _____

2. What might account for differences between the rates of deceased and
   living donors in a particular country?

   _____

3. Should donation permission be assumed when people die or should
   people have to register on an organ-donor list beforehand?

   _____

4. In what situations would you consider becoming a living organ donor?

   _____

B. Discuss the questions and your answers, first with a partner, then in a group.

A. Below are key words and phrases you will hear in Listening 1. Check the words you understand. Then, check the words you use.

	UNDERSTAND	USE		UNDERSTAND	USE
captive audience (n.)	☐	☐	in vitro fertilization (n.)	☐	☐
cervical cancer (n.)	☐	☐	lymph nodes (n.)	☐	☐
charred (adj.)	☐	☐	metastasized (v.)	☐	☐
contaminated (adj.)	☐	☐	minuscule (adj.)	☐	☐
cutting-edge (adj.)	☐	☐	morgue (n.)	☐	☐
gynecology (n.)	☐	☐	pain management (n.)	☐	☐
immortal (adj.)	☐	☐	prostate cancer (n.)	☐	☐
immunity (n.)	☐	☐	radium (n.)	☐	☐
informed consent (n.)	☐	☐	sampling (n.)	☐	☐
invasive (adj.)	☐	☐	tumour (n.)	☐	☐

B. Write a definition for each of the words or phrases you do not understand, using a dictionary and continuing on a separate sheet of paper if necessary.

WORD/PHRASE	DEFINITION

C. Complete the following paragraph using words and phrases from task A.

No one is _____, but with proper health care, people can lead long lives. A _____ that is caught early enough, before it has _____, can sometimes be removed without _____ surgery, in which a _____ incision needs to be made. This is particularly true of _____ in women and _____ in men. However, when a cancer is not caught early enough, a doctor can offer little relief other than _____.

D. The expression *informed consent* refers to a person's agreement to a medical procedure after being made aware of all the potential consequences. At what age would you consider a person old enough to offer his or her informed consent for each of the following procedures? Explain your answers.

PROCEDURE	AGE	EXPLANATION
getting a tattoo		
undergoing cosmetic surgery		
getting a vaccination		
giving blood		
donating an organ		
donating one's body after death		
giving consent to life-saving surgery		
opting out of life-saving surgery		

E. Working in a small group, share and discuss your answers to task D. Look for consensus on opinions you have in common.

Conducting an Interview

In court, it's said that good lawyers never ask questions to which they don't know the answers. Interviews are different: it's all right to be surprised. However, conducting an interview should be more like a conversation between equals than a series of questions from an interviewer who doesn't contribute to the discussion. Good interviews are based as much on the preparation of the interviewer as on the knowledge and expertise of the person being interviewed. In the questions below, it's clear that the interviewer, Anna Maria Tremonti, has researched the topic and is able to add to the conversation by offering details she would like the interviewee to expand on.

A. Read the following excerpts from Listening 1 and consider the function of each of the questions. Which are likely to elicit the least information and which, the most? Rank them from 1 (least) to 4 (most).

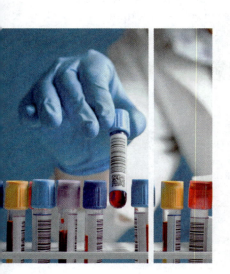

QUESTION	QUESTION FUNCTION	RANK
Well, let's begin with the woman herself. Who *was* Henrietta?	**A:** An opening statement + a simple information question help introduce a topic.	
Well you describe in graphic detail the lead-up to her death. Tell us about that cancer.	**B:** A statement + an open-ended question elicit a more detailed answer.	
And in fact you describe how the woman in the lab just went, you know, "Here we go again, this isn't going to work." And then what happened?	**C:** A recap statement + an open-ended question create a narrative structure, telling part of the story and then letting the interviewee tell the rest.	
This is the Salk vaccine?	**D:** A close-ended yes/no question in context requests confirmation or clarification.	

B. Read the following excerpts, also from Listening 1, and indicate which function (as noted in task A) each question has.

❶ "Coloured" in quotation marks—that's what they called it, right? ___D___

❷ ... you say that the researchers were trying to grow cells, and so they took her cells. What were they hoping to get from those cells? _____

❸ So when they first took her cells, it was just another cell sampling? _____

❹ So they knew her cells were very different before she died? _____

❺ So when she died, what did they do? _____

❻ Tell us more, then, about the way Henrietta Lacks' cells *were* used in research and *are* used in research. _____

❼ And of course, they didn't call them Henrietta cells; what did they call them? _____

❽ What happened with that experiment at Ohio State Penitentiary? _____

❾ To see what they would do? _____

❿ What year was that? _____

> To say something is "in quotation marks" is to emphasize that it was said or written by someone else and that it was not necessarily your own idea or opinion.

C. Write a question that illustrates each of the functions described in task A, using vocabulary you have learned in the chapter so far. Then, with a partner, practise asking and answering your questions.

QUESTION FUNCTION	EXAMPLE
A: An opening statement + a simple information question help introduce a topic.	*Prostate cancer occurs in one organ of the body. What has happened when a cancer has metastasized?*
B: A statement + an open-ended question elicit a more detailed answer.	
C: A recap statement + an open-ended question create a narrative structure, telling part of the story and then letting the interviewee tell the rest.	
D: A close-ended yes/no question in context requests confirmation or clarification.	

LISTENING ❶   The Immortal Life of Henrietta Lacks

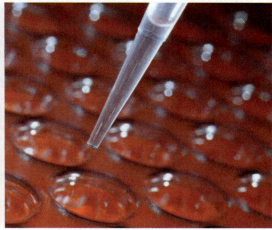

An unintentional donor of tumour cells has found posthumous fame, thanks to science writer Rebecca Skloot and her book *The Immortal Life of Henrietta Lacks*. In the book, Skloot describes how cells taken from Lacks' body formed the foundation of countless medical advances, while Lacks and her family were neither consulted nor informed. In this interview, Tremonti asks Skloot about Henrietta Lacks' story and some of its consequences.

Before You Listen

Taking Lacks' cancerous tumour cells and using them for research at the time violated no laws; the cells were considered medical waste. However, the law surrounding the extraction of additional cells from other organs of her body was less clear. One thing that is certain is the enormous extent to which research based on Lacks' cells has made medical improvements possible.

Based on what you understand about Lacks' contribution to science, discuss the following questions in a group.

• Do you think Lacks' living relatives should be compensated in some way?

• Would laws guaranteeing such compensation affect medical research in the future? How?

• Would compensation encourage a black-market trade of cells and organs?

While You Listen

The first time you listen, try to get the general idea. Listen a second time and take notes on Skloot's response to each question or prompt from the interviewer. Listen a third time to check your notes and add details.

QUESTIONS/PROMPTS	NOTES
Well, let's begin with the woman herself. Who *was* Henrietta?	
"Coloured" in quotation marks—that's what they called it, right?	
Well you describe in graphic detail the lead-up to her death. Tell us about that cancer.	
And you, you actually describe the treatment. They used—a reminder of how far we've come—they were using radium in glass tubes, and they would stitch it inside the body for like a day or two—or …	
So she was going through all of this pain, and she died. And you say that the researchers were trying to grow cells, and so they took her cells. What were they hoping to get from those cells?	
So when they first took her cells, it was just another cell sampling? … you describe how the woman in the lab just went, you know, "Here we go again, this isn't going to work." And then what happened?	
So they knew her cells were very different before she died? … So when she died, what did they do?	
Tell us more, then, about the way Henrietta Lacks' cells *were* used in research and *are* used in research.	
This is the Salk vaccine?	
And of course, they didn't call them Henrietta cells; what did they call them?	
What happened with that experiment at Ohio State Penitentiary?	

QUESTIONS/PROMPTS	NOTES
Was the very idea of, "Yeah, go ahead and inject me, you can watch the cancer grow, you can take it off and watch it again."	
To see what they would do?	
What year was that?	
It's incredible. I mean, the research that you have done sort of exposes everyone to the realities of those decades ago that—we forget how medical research was done.	

After You Listen

During World War II, Nazi doctors and scientists conducted horrific research on human prisoners, including sterilizing men and women, infecting healthy people with dangerous diseases to test vaccines and freezing people to study the effects of hypothermia and the best revival techniques. After the experiments, prisoners were usually killed so they could be dissected. Though completely cruel and unethical, some of this systematic research provided findings that would be enormously helpful to the medical profession today.

Form a group of four or more students, then divide into two subgroups and, taking opposing positions, debate whether the medical benefits of using information gained from such research outweigh the ethical concerns about how it was obtained.

VOCABULARY BUILD

A. Below are key words and phrases you will hear in Listening 2 or Listening 3. Check the words you understand. Then, check the words you use.

	UNDERSTAND	USE		UNDERSTAND	USE
ailment (n.)	☐	☐	macabre (adj.)	☐	☐
apprehension (n.)	☐	☐	millennia (n.)	☐	☐
compiled* (v.)	☐	☐	murky (adj.)	☐	☐
comply (v.)	☐	☐	pin down (v.)	☐	☐
en masse (adv.)	☐	☐	plastinates (n.)	☐	☐
fair game (n.)	☐	☐	rabies (n.)	☐	☐
heavy metal poisoning (n.)	☐	☐	sentiment (n.)	☐	☐
invalid (n.)	☐	☐	toxicological (adj.)	☐	☐
lay people (n.)	☐	☐	tribute (n.)	☐	☐
locums (n.)	☐	☐	trolling (v.)	☐	☐

*Appears on the Academic Word List

B. Write a definition for each of the words or phrases you do not understand, using a dictionary and continuing on a separate sheet of paper if necessary.

WORD/PHRASE	DEFINITION

C. Heteronyms are words that are spelled the same way but have different meanings and pronunciations. *Invalid*, with stress on the first syllable, is a noun describing a person made weak by injury or illness. *Invalid*, with stress on the second syllable, is an adjective describing something not recognized or not legal. Write sentences for the following words and underline the stressed syllable in each heteronym.

1 subject (n.): _____

_____

subject (v.): _____

_____

2 present (n.): _____

_____

present (v.): _____

_____

3 suspect (n.): _____

_____

suspect (v.): _____

_____

D. Many people feel uncomfortable at even the mention of blood, dissection or medical procedures. Write a paragraph explaining your feelings. Use at least seven words or phrases from task A.

_____

_____

_____

_____

_____

_____

_____

_____

_____

_____

Web+ Visit the Companion Website to complete a vocabulary review exercise for this chapter.

E. Share your paragraph with a partner. Do you both feel the same way or do you react differently? Discuss your reactions.

LISTENING ②

In the Dissection Room

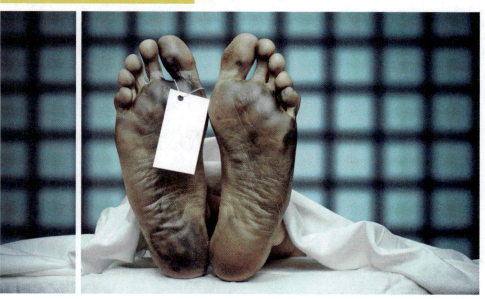

Most jobs require practical training in which the trainee is allowed to make mistakes. However, no one wants a trainee doctor making mistakes during an operation, so dissection of cadavers—dead bodies—provides medical students with in-depth knowledge of how the body is structured and how various organs, bones, nerves, muscles and blood vessels can be identified and accessed during an operation.

Although there are now plastic models and computer simulations available to help students learn about anatomy, many medical professionals feel that simulations cannot compare with dissecting a human cadaver.

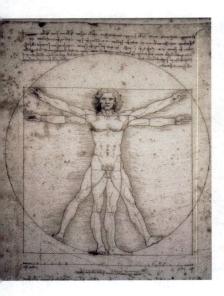

Before You Listen

Here is the opening segment of Listening 2. Based on this introduction, write three questions you would expect to hear and try to predict the answers.

> "For thousands of years, people have been studying and documenting human anatomy. In these days, we do it to turn out well-trained physicians and surgeons. Students traditionally use bodies donated for dissections, as well as prosections, which are expertly prepared specimens that reveal the important structures they need to know about. But increasingly, medical schools are abandoning the dissection approach to teaching anatomy. So, I went along to one place that still does it this way—that's Cambridge University—to find out what their students think of the process."

QUESTION: _____

ANSWER: _____

QUESTION: _____

ANSWER: _____

QUESTION: _____

ANSWER: _____

While You Listen

There are two podcasts in this listening. In the first, Chris Smith, doctor and clinical lecturer in virology at Cambridge University, listens while clinical anatomist Theo Welch takes his students through a dissection. Smith gets reactions from the students and then interviews surgeon George Marsden and clinical anatomist Chris Constant. While you listen, take notes on what both the professionals and the students say about dissections and the value of body donations.

SPEAKER	NOTES
Theo Welch and students	
Abigail Lucas	
Lahiru [Handunnepthi]	
Lucas	
George Marsden	

SPEAKER	NOTES
Chris Constant	
Rowan DeSouza	*First-year medical student, Clare College, Cambridge*
Claire Blackman	
Constant	
Constant	*Anyone can donate their body, but there are criteria.*
Constant	*All the parts remain together; not mixed.*
Constant	*Donating is a generous, feel-good act.*

In the second podcast, writer Kat Arney interviews physician and filmmaker Paul Trotman about his film *Donated to Science*. In it, Trotman followed three donors to document their reasons for donating their bodies to science and he talks about the impact their decisions have had on medical students. While you listen, number the steps in Trotman's procedure in the correct order.

Trotman ...

___1___ qualified as a doctor;

_____ contacted potential donors willing to be the subjects of a film;

_____ had thirty student volunteers, narrowed these down to twenty, then ended up with ten;

_____ interviewed patients shortly before their deaths;

_____ interviewed students after they had finished their dissections;

_____ made a film about becoming an organ donor;

_____ narrowed the list of potential film subjects to six and then three people;

_____ observed students dissecting the bodies;

_____ proposed making a film about donating one's body to medical school;

_____ spent six months applying to the ethics committee for permission;

_____ started making films on medical themes;

___12___ showed students the interviews he had conducted with the donors.

After You Listen

Does the content of these two podcasts make you interested in seeing Trotman's film? Why or why not? Make notes and then discuss your answer with a partner.

_____

_____

_____

_____

Academic
Survival Skill

Practising the Harkness Method

Edward Harkness (1874–1940) was a philanthropist who gave money to various charities and who supported museums, hospitals and schools. In 1930, he proposed a teaching innovation to do away with the teacher-fronted classroom, in which a teacher lectures students sitting in rows. His idea was to seat a teacher and a dozen students around an oval table so they could all make eye contact. As part of the seminar-style instruction, students were asked to come prepared to speak on a topic and take control of their own discussion, asking and answering questions and thereby developing their discussion skills.

A. Read the following definitions of the Harkness discussion skills and match each statement to the appropriate skill.

DISCUSSION SKILLS	STATEMENTS
❶ ANALYZING: breaking an idea down into its key parts	_4_ A cadaver is a corpse that is intended for medical use or scientific study.
❷ APPLYING: showing how an idea can be put into practice	_2_ A medical professional can offer a retrodiagnosis simply by examining the observations about someone's death.
❸ CHALLENGING: taking a point of view on an idea that is different from someone else's point of view	_3_ I disagree with the idea that hospitals may automatically assume everyone is an organ donor.
❹ DEFINING: providing the meaning of an idea, term or principle	_5_ I think I can show what a tumour is by using an example.
❺ EXPLAINING: illustrating an idea or principle ✓	_8_ If people are reluctant to donate an organ, it might be due to a misunderstanding of the procedure.
❻ ORGANIZING: arranging the flow of the seminar	_7_ If we compare retrodiagnosis to hands-on diagnosis of a present-day patient, we see in both cases that a doctor simply tries to gather as much information as possible.
❼ RELATING: showing how one idea has something in common with another	_9_ Maybe people didn't understand rabies when Edgar Allan Poe died.
❽ SIMPLIFYING: making complex ideas easier to ✓ understand	_6_ Perhaps we could move on to the next topic now.
❾ SUGGESTING: offering an idea	_10_ So we've now covered the process of dissection and what happens to the cadaver afterwards.
❿ SUMMARIZING: putting together the most important points	_1_ Toxicological testing could be achieved through the chemical analysis of skin, hair or organs.

B. Read the following statements from Listening 3 and consider how you would address them depending on the different skill you might use in a seminar discussion. Choose one skill for each statement and write your responses.

1 Our ability to diagnose and treat disease continues to improve.

_____

_____

_____

2 And [historical accounts and eyewitness interpretations] have a lot of problems with them, these sorts of historical documents, because in some cases they were compiled hundreds of years after somebody died, so that in some cases they're as much legend as fact.

_____

_____

_____

3 Some people feel that the dead do have a right to privacy, ...

_____

_____

_____

4 He said what historians are really interested in is what the person's life was like: how they suffered, their symptoms, things like that.

_____

_____

_____

C. With a partner, practise reading the statements and your responses from task B.

WARM-UP ASSIGNMENT
Prepare for a Seminar

Seminars differ from lectures, and other classes, in that students are expected to be highly prepared and ready to interact, present information and ask and answer questions. In this assignment, you will prepare and deliver a brief presentation and then take questions from a group of four to six students.

A. The general seminar topic is the implications of donating one's body to science. In addition, your presentation should include a subtopic based on issues related to one of the following: culture, ethics, legal concerns or religion. Consult with your classmates to ensure that each subtopic is covered by some students in the class.

> The word "seminar" comes from the Latin for "breeding ground"; it is used in the sense of "helping ideas to grow."

Visit the Companion Website to learn more about common citation and referencing guidelines.

B. Do your research. Use at least one online source (other than *Wikipedia*) and one source from the library. Keep complete records of each source, following the citation and referencing guidelines of your discipline. As you do your research, keep in mind the discussion skills of the Harkness method and use them to anticipate questions and prepare answers.

SUBTOPIC: _____

DISCUSSION SKILLS	QUESTIONS	ANSWERS
ANALYZING		
APPLYING		
CHALLENGING		
DEFINING		
EXPLAINING		
ORGANIZING		
RELATING		
SIMPLIFYING		
SUGGESTING		
SUMMARIZING		

C. Prepare notes for your presentation that introduce your subtopic and what you have learned.

D. Write your key points on cue cards. Practise your presentation with a partner, who should be prepared to comment and ask questions. Take note of your partner's comments and questions.

E. Form a group of four to six students and deliver your presentation. Ask and answer questions in the group.

Listening for Paraphrase

When speaking, people often repeat themselves. Sometimes this repetition comes from a conscious need to identify and emphasize key points. In other cases, a speaker may repeat ideas unconsciously. Repetition is often done through paraphrasing, in which the speaker shares the same information using different words. When taking notes during interviews in particular, it is important to identify a key point the first time it is made and to see whether subsequent repetition has a purpose—such as offering additional information or emphasis—or whether it is redundant.

A. Read the following excerpts from the Chris Constant interview in Listening 2. Consider the speaker's key points, how and why he uses paraphrasing and how effective it is.

"Cost" is repeated in "costly." In the paraphrase, more information is given, identifying organization as the expensive part of a program.

"Effort" is expanded on with "time-consuming" and "demanding."

"A number of reasons: <u>cost</u> is one, the <u>effort</u> it takes to run a body donation program, ethical and legal issues, the difficult issues of respect—and basically the organization of such a program is actually very <u>costly</u>, very <u>time-consuming</u> and very <u>demanding</u> in every way, ..."

"Anyone can donate their body after death. However, when the time comes, we have <u>certain criteria with which we have to comply</u>, and there are <u>certain criteria which result in our having to reject someone's remains</u>. The donors are aware of that when they sign a consent form, that there is a possibility that <u>their remains would not be accepted</u>."

"Certain criteria ..." is repeated, but in the second phrase, the result of applying the criteria is explained.

The phrase "... reject someone's remains" is paraphrased with "their remains would not be accepted." The latter phrase is a less harsh way of explaining what might happen.

"To begin with, all the parts remain together for each individual donor's remains. <u>They are not mixed</u> so that they are all returned to one particular coffin and then <u>cremated or buried in accordance with the donor's wishes</u>. Prior to that, we have a committal service here in the anatomy centre, in the dissecting room, at which students and others involved in dissection attend. The identities of the donors become known to these students. They have a chance to pay their last respects and indeed write a tribute to each of the donors, upon whom they have worked over the previous academic year. And it's actually quite a moving event. By the time we're finished with the remains, they are respectfully <u>buried or cremated in accordance with the wishes of the donor</u>, and everyone has their own remains. <u>There's no mixing of parts</u>."

"They are not mixed" is paraphrased in "There's no mixing of parts." The purpose is to re-emphasize this important point after many other ideas are discussed.

"Cremated or buried ..." is repeated below in "buried or cremated ..." Word order changes, but no new information is added. The function of this paraphrase is to return to the main topic and emphasize the idea so it is clear to the listener.

B. When speaking without prepared notes, people may repeat themselves unconsciously, leading to redundancy. Read the excerpt from Listening 2 on the next page and look for examples of redundancy. Cross out unnecessary repetition.

"Well, I would be very encouraging [about people donating their bodies]. First of all, it's an extremely generous act. It is something one can feel very good about. It benefits the students and, ultimately, the doctors that are made from the students, and therefore the patients in years to come. So what the donors are doing now in their lifetime, to be carried out on their death, will benefit generations to come. I would be very positive. I think it's a great thing to do, and I think you can feel you've benefited people after the good you do in life has finally come to an end."

C. Reread your edited passage and write the key points in one or two sentences.

_____

_____

_____

D. Imagine your answer to task C is the opening of a talk. Now imagine you have completed your talk and want to conclude by paraphrasing your opening statements. Write a paraphrase of your opening sentence(s).

_____

_____

_____

Investigating the Ills of Long-Dead Celebrities

There is an enduring fascination with the lives of long-dead historical figures. For example, thousands of biographies have been written about Napoleon Bonaparte (1769–1821). Finding new information about such figures is often extremely difficult, but new interpretations of their lives and deaths may arise when modern medical knowledge, such as DNA testing, is added to historical observations and medical records.

Before You Listen

In the following excerpt from Sarah Crespi's interview with *Science* writer Sam Kean, she opens the discussion of "retrodiagnosis," or "retrospective diagnosis."

"Our ability to diagnose and treat disease continues to improve. And along with the advancing understanding of ourselves comes a desire to know more about those who came before us. In 'retrodiagnosis,' doctors use current methods, like genetics, combined with historical accounts to examine illness and death among the dead and famous."

Besides general interest, what might be the point of retrodiagnosis? For example, how might it help modern medical research or our understanding of history?

_____

_____

_____

Here are some of the famous individuals who have been studied in retrodiagnosis conferences. Find out more about the ones you are not familiar with. Which of these people are you most interested in? Why? Discuss your findings —and your answers—in a group.

- Akhenaten, Egyptian pharaoh
- Alexander the Great, Greek conqueror
- Ludwig van Beethoven, German composer
- Simón Bolívar, Latin American liberator
- Christopher Columbus, Italian explorer
- Claudius, Roman emperor
- George A. Custer, American soldier
- King Herod, Roman statesman
- John Paul Jones, founder of the American navy
- Abraham Lincoln, American president
- Wolfgang Amadeus Mozart, Austrian composer
- Florence Nightingale, English nurse
- Pericles, Greek statesman
- Edgar Allan Poe, American writer
- Heinrich Schliemann, German archaeologist
- Booker T. Washington, American educator

While You Listen

The first time you listen, try to get the general idea. Listen a second time and take notes on each segment. Focus on the main messages and consider whether the explanations and examples support the speaker's main ideas. Listen a third time to check your notes and add details.

SEGMENT	NOTES
I spoke with *Science* contributing correspondent Sam Kean about a yearly conference that focuses on investigating the mysterious deaths of the likes of Christopher Columbus and King Herod.	
So, what kind, what kind of criteria do make it worthwhile to look back and figure out how someone died maybe a hundred years ago?	
So what kind of evidence is fair game in this retrodiagnosis process?	
Well, it seems like—regardless of our improving technology—that it would be pretty hard to diagnose someone who's been long dead. Are there any good examples of, you know, a death where we can say, oh, this case has been solved?	

SEGMENT	NOTES
So how about an example of deaths where the person's famous, they've died, but there's just no way we're ever going to know. Is that something that these retrodiagnosers also decide, that it's impossible to tell?	*There are many proposed diagnoses, including narcolepsy, agoraphobia, lupus, pigeon allergies and lactose intolerance. Diagnoses are more difficult the longer someone has been dead, e.g., King Herod (74–44 BCE).*
So, are there any ethical concerns about exposing medical conditions in people who have died, even if it was a long time ago?	
So, is this something that historians are also finding useful? It sounds like this is mostly the practice of these doctors.	

After You Listen

Imagine you are the descendant of a famous person, such as Charles Darwin, who was the subject of a retrodiagnosis conference. What kind of information, possibly revealed by your relative's medical records, might you be concerned about? Write notes and then discuss your answers in a group.

_____

_____

_____

_____

_____

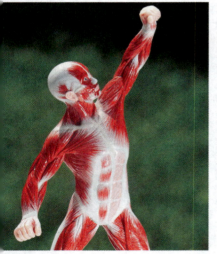

FINAL ASSIGNMENT
Take Part in a Seminar

Now it's your turn. Use everything you have learned in this chapter to research and participate in a seminar of one hour or longer.

A. The topic of the seminar is the implications of donating one's body to science. Form four groups based on the subtopics you and your classmates chose for the Warm-Up Assignment (page 139): culture, ethics, legal concerns or religion. Continue with the subtopic you had already researched, but this time in greater detail and in a group.

GROUP SUBTOPIC: _____

B. As a group, compare and combine information from each group member's Warm-Up Assignment. If necessary, conduct additional research in the library and online.

C. Anticipate questions students in other groups are likely to ask and prepare answers. Use the question functions from the Focus on Speaking (page 130) and the Harkness discussion skills from the Academic Survival Skill (page 138) to help you.

D. Plan your group's part in the seminar. Use the following table to organize your notes.

SEMINAR STRUCTURE	NOTES
Introduce your subtopic.	
Explain why it is important.	
Provide background on the issues.	
Anticipate questions from members of other groups.	
Answer anticipated questions.	

E. Divide the speaking points among group members and, after practising, participate in the overall class seminar. As each group talks, take notes and be prepared to ask and answer questions.

F. Afterwards, discuss the seminar as a group and evaluate points and presentations that were the most successful and those that could have been better.

"Science cannot resolve moral conflicts, but it can help to more accurately frame the debates around these conflicts."
—Heinz R. Pagels, theoretical physicist (1939–1988)

CHAPTER 8

Saving Planet Earth

Despite all the time and energy put into space exploration, the only home most of us are ever likely to know is the planet we live on now. For this reason, you would think that we would be more concerned about controlling changes to Earth's climate, preserving its natural resources and conserving its countless species. **But small and large decisions made by individuals, businesses and governments are making the world less able to support us, particularly as the human population continues to grow.**

Because of overharvesting, climate change and shrinking habitats, some mammals, fish, birds, insects and plants are becoming extinct. By eliminating one part of a food chain, it's likely that each extinction will lead to others.

In this chapter, you will

- listen to an interview about endangered species, extinction and environmental ethics, and watch two excerpts from a lecture about sustaining life on Earth;

- learn vocabulary related to species extinction and environmental ethics and activism;

- practise signposting to help guide listeners from one idea to another;

- focus on interpreting audience questions;

- learn discussion techniques for examining problems;

- practise speaking individually, in pairs and in groups;

- introduce a speaker and take part in a town hall meeting.

GEARING UP

The International Union for Conservation of Nature (IUCN) estimates that more than 800 species have become extinct in the last 500 years, and thousands more are threatened.

A. Consider the chart, which illustrates the extinction risk for 47,677 species, and answer the questions that follow.

Proportion of species in different threat categories

Source: Convention on Biological Diversity. (2010). Proportion of species in different threat categories. Retrieved from http://www.cbd.int/gbo3/?pub=6667&section=6691

① *Data deficient* means we don't know enough about some species. However, we do know the percentage of species that are clearly threatened.

What percentage is it? _____

② What does *extinct* or *extinct in the wild* mean?

_____

③ Many mammals are at risk in South and Southeast Asia. Why?

_____

_____

④ What factors might be endangering species in other parts of the world?

_____

_____

B. Discuss the questions and your answers, first with a partner, then in a group.

A. Below are key words and phrases you will hear in Listening 1. Check the words you understand. Then, check the words you use.

	UNDERSTAND	USE		UNDERSTAND	USE
abdicating (v.)	☐	☐	micro-organism (n.)	☐	☐
carrot and the stick (n.)	☐	☐	migration* (n.)	☐	☐
empowering (v.)	☐	☐	morality (n.)	☐	☐
endangered species (n.)	☐	☐	mosaic (n.)	☐	☐
escalated (v.)	☐	☐	obligation (n.)	☐	☐
habitat (n.)	☐	☐	potentially (adv.)	☐	☐
insignificant* (adj.)	☐	☐	provocative (adj.)	☐	☐
interconnection (n.)	☐	☐	strand (n.)	☐	☐
interrelatedness (n.)	☐	☐	triage (n.)	☐	☐
last call (n.)	☐	☐	win-win-win situation (n.)	☐	☐

*Appears on the Academic Word List

B. Write a definition for each of the words or phrases you do not understand, using a dictionary and continuing on a separate sheet of paper if necessary.

WORD/PHRASE	DEFINITION

C. New words can be formed from other words by adding a prefix and a suffix, such as in *interrelatedness* and *interconnection*.

For each of the words in the following table, add the prefix *inter-* and, from the word box, choose an appropriate suffix. In some cases, the last letter of the original word may need to be dropped, so check your spelling. Then, use each new word in a sentence. The first one has been done for you as an example.

-ability	-ally	-ency	-ity	-ize
-al	-ary	-ent	-ive	-ship

ORIGINAL WORD	NEW WORD	SENTENCE
act	*interactive*	*The interactive computer responds to voice commands.*
change		
culture		
depend		
discipline		
government		
national		
relation		

D. In its 2012 Red List, the IUCN identified 4,088 species as "critically endangered," including the greater bamboo lemur, the Javan rhino, the Liben lark, the Yangtze giant softshell turtle and the Seychelles sheath-tailed bat. Choose a species and write a paragraph explaining why that species is endangered. In your paragraph, use seven words or phrases from task A.

_____

_____

_____

_____

_____

_____

_____

_____

E. Working in a small group, read and discuss your paragraphs. Identify common causes endangering different species. Discuss what can be done to save each.

As a young girl, ethologist Jane Goodall was fascinated with animals and yearned to travel to Africa. Shortly after she turned eighteen, she travelled to Tanzania and met scientist Louis Leakey, who persuaded her to take on a long-term study of chimpanzees. Goodall lived near the primates and observed them for decades. Her work led to many insights into chimpanzee behaviour. Goodall now oversees a variety of conservation and education projects worldwide. In Listening 1, she is interviewed by Anna Maria Tremonti.

Before You Listen

Read the following excerpt from the introduction to Goodall's interview, in which Tremonti talks about Goodall's recent work and concerns.

"Those are Hainan gibbons making those otherworldly calls. Conservationists believe it's close to the last call for the primates. They're found only in the shrinking forests of China's Hainan Island. The gibbons are one of the animals on a new list of the world's one hundred most endangered species. Perhaps few of us would actually miss the dusky gopher frog or the northern bald ibis or Nelson's small-eared shrew. But the report [from IUCN] asks a provocative question: are all these species nevertheless priceless or—worthless? Are they priceless in and of themselves, or some just not worth as much of our concern and conservation efforts than other species?"

It would be ideal if we could save every species, but resources for conservation efforts are often limited. Which of the following endangered species would you choose to save? In making your decision, what criteria will you apply? Why?

stag beetle
(*Lucanus cervus*)

giant panda
(*Ailuropoda melanoleuca*)

pitcher plant
(*Nepenthes alata*)

_____
_____
_____
_____
_____
_____

An "ethologist" studies animal behaviour; an "ethnologist" studies human behaviour.

While You Listen

The first time you listen, try to get the general idea. Listen a second time and take notes on each segment. Focus on the main message and consider whether the explanations and examples support the speaker's main ideas. Listen a third time to check your notes and add details.

SEGMENT	NOTES
What are your thoughts about the question posed by that report: priceless or worthless?	*Goodall disagrees that species are worthless.*
What are some of your favourite examples of species brought back from the brink of extinction?	*The northern bald ibis is one favourite.*
What kind of ethical duties do humans have to save endangered species?	
… Some argue that we need to do some triage and focus our resources on certain species.	
Again that—the fact that everything is woven together and you can't separate. And you almost are saying that we have to work backwards: you want to save the big one, then even the tiniest spore matters in that chain.	
Well, what you're really talking about then is an ethical obligation that we have to more generally look at species and ecosystems of all kinds?	
… Well, on another ethical front, the Jane Goodall Institute just released the results of a survey on Canadian attitudes toward the use of chimpanzees in entertainment. Tell us about that.	
The survey also found most Canadians are concerned about chimpanzees possibly becoming extinct, but how much are they willing to do to protect chimpanzee habitat or prevent the poaching of chimps?	
Do animals have rights?	
So in other words, we are not necessarily violating animal rights, but we are abdicating our responsibility if our action—or inaction—creates a situation where they go extinct?	
… Biodiversity and endangered species are just one environmental issue that has been framed in ethical terms. Al Gore, for example, has famously described climate change as a moral issue. What do you think?	
How much do you believe that people believe that environmental issues are moral or ethical issues?	*Roots and Shoots, a program for young people in 130 countries, is helping raise awareness.*

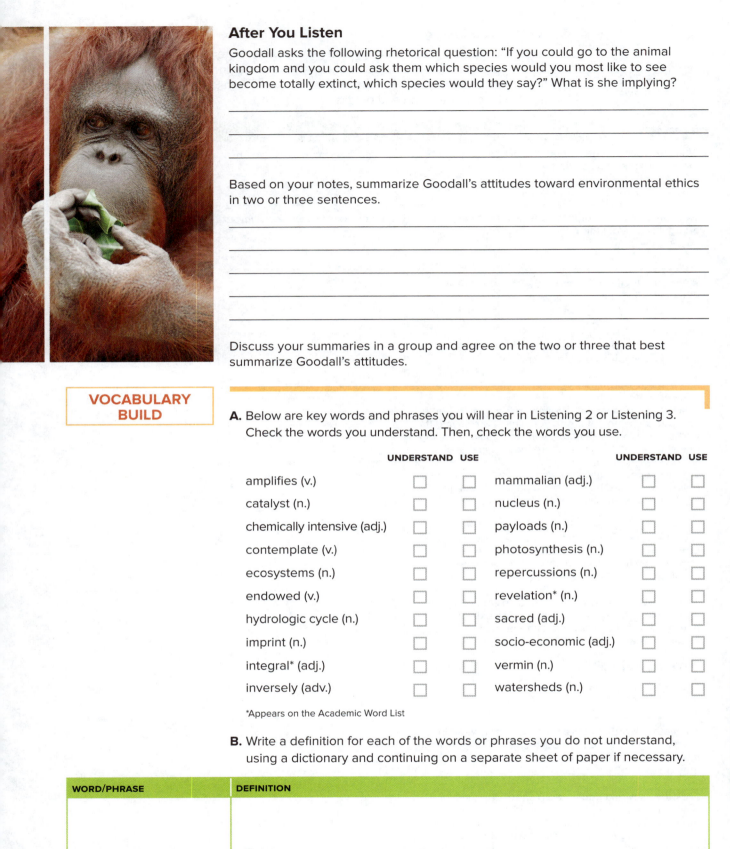

After You Listen

Goodall asks the following rhetorical question: "If you could go to the animal kingdom and you could ask them which species would you most like to see become totally extinct, which species would they say?" What is she implying?

_____

_____

_____

Based on your notes, summarize Goodall's attitudes toward environmental ethics in two or three sentences.

_____

_____

_____

_____

_____

Discuss your summaries in a group and agree on the two or three that best summarize Goodall's attitudes.

VOCABULARY BUILD

A. Below are key words and phrases you will hear in Listening 2 or Listening 3. Check the words you understand. Then, check the words you use.

	UNDERSTAND	USE		UNDERSTAND	USE
amplifies (v.)	☐	☐	mammalian (adj.)	☐	☐
catalyst (n.)	☐	☐	nucleus (n.)	☐	☐
chemically intensive (adj.)	☐	☐	payloads (n.)	☐	☐
contemplate (v.)	☐	☐	photosynthesis (n.)	☐	☐
ecosystems (n.)	☐	☐	repercussions (n.)	☐	☐
endowed (v.)	☐	☐	revelation* (n.)	☐	☐
hydrologic cycle (n.)	☐	☐	sacred (adj.)	☐	☐
imprint (n.)	☐	☐	socio-economic (adj.)	☐	☐
integral* (adj.)	☐	☐	vermin (n.)	☐	☐
inversely (adv.)	☐	☐	watersheds (n.)	☐	☐

*Appears on the Academic Word List

B. Write a definition for each of the words or phrases you do not understand, using a dictionary and continuing on a separate sheet of paper if necessary.

WORD/PHRASE	DEFINITION

WORD/PHRASE	DEFINITION

C. Consider the words *ecosystem, hydrologic, photosynthesis* and *socio-economic*. Write what each of the prefixes means and find another word that contains it. Define each word, using a dictionary if necessary. Then, use each word in a sentence.

PREFIX	MEANING	WORD	DEFINITION
eco-			
hydro-			
photo-			
socio-			

1. _____
_____
2. _____
_____
3. _____
_____
4. _____
_____

D. Complete the following paragraph, using words and phrases from task A.

No matter how carefully we contemplate our actions, each of us makes a large

_____ on the environment. Even the smallest actions can

have serious _____. Consider a plastic bottle of water:

plastics are manufactured via _____ processes. When

discarded, plastic enters different _____, polluting

_____ and threatening the survival of species. In the desert,

thirsty camels find discarded water bottles and swallow them, choking to death.

_____ feeding on the camel corpses may spread disease.

Widespread disease affects _____ opportunities as live-

stock and workers become sick. A single piece of plastic can become the

_____ that changes the web of life.

E. Working in a small group, read and discuss the paragraph in task D. How might discarded plastic damage your environment?

LISTENING ❷

The Legacy: An Elder's Vision for Our Sustainable Future, Part 1

In the first of two excerpts from a speech given in Perth, Australia, award-winning scientist, environmental activist and presenter David Suzuki talks about people's impact on the natural world, particularly in the destruction of other species and their habitats. Born in 1936, Suzuki now sees his role as that of an elder and shares the wisdom he has acquired after a lifetime of considering—and combatting—environmental problems.

Before You Listen

Read the excerpt from Suzuki's introduction on the next page. In it, he establishes his expertise, comments on scientific process, outlines an accomplishment, explains a revelation and suggests a shift in attitude.

"I spent thirty years as a geneticist. And one of the most astounding things to me has been the way that scientists have accumulated techniques, methodology, to analyze DNA, the genetic material. And in 2001, geneticists announced the completion of the Human Genome Project, the delineation of all three billion letters in the DNA of a single human nucleus. It was an astounding achievement, and to me, the most incredible insight that came from the Human Genome Project was a revelation that 99 percent of the genes in our cells are identical to the genes in chimpanzees. They *are* our nearest relatives. The revelation that each of us carries tens of thousands of genes identical to the genes in our pet dogs and cats, identical to the genes in eagles, salmon, fruit flies, dandelions and cedar trees. All of life is related to us through a common evolutionary history. And surely if the rest of creation is our relatives, they deserve to be treated with greater respect and care than if we simply regard them as resources—as pests, as weeds, or vermin."

Write brief notes from the excerpt on the following topics.

SUZUKI'S EXPERTISE: _____

SCIENTIFIC PROCESS: _____

_____

ACCOMPLISHMENT: _____

_____

REVELATION: _____

_____

SHIFT IN ATTITUDE: _____

Suzuki's shift in attitude might be interpreted as anything from making simple changes in one's lifestyle to not using other species as resources in any way. In a group, discuss your attitudes about using other species for food and clothing.

While You Listen

When you're listening to a lecture, it's difficult to identify "paragraphs," which you can easily do when reading. However, there are natural breaks in a speech as the speaker moves from one topic to another. The following are the topic sentences that begin each segment of this excerpt. The first time you listen, try to get the general idea. Listen a second time and take notes on each segment. Listen a third time to check your notes and add details.

TOPIC SENTENCE	NOTES
And in an act of incredible generosity, the web of living things that are our relatives create, cleanse and replenish the most fundamental needs that we have as animals.	*Plants created the oxygen-rich atmosphere we depend on. Life is a critical part of the hydrologic cycle; water covers 70 percent of the planet: it evaporates, forms clouds, rains on the land, runs into rivers, lakes and oceans and evaporates.*
And all life is a—sorry—every bit of our food that we eat for our nutrition, to create our bodies, was once alive.	*Photosynthesis:*
We boast that we are intelligent ...	

TOPIC SENTENCE	NOTES
Scientists can also use DNA in very clever ways to trace the movement of humanity across the planet.	*150,000 years ago, our species was born in Africa, alongside the woolly mammoths, sabre-toothed tigers, giant moa birds and sloths.*
Now you gotta admit, when you think of us in that context, we weren't very impressive.	
Of course, the reason we were so undistinguished was that our secret was hidden.	
In only 150,000 years, that strategy worked and brought us to a complete position of dominance.	*10,000 years ago, start of Agricultural Revolution:* *8,000 years later:* *Less than 2,000 years later:* *200 years later:*
There's a simple rule in biology: that a population number of a given species is inversely related to its physical size.	
We are now the most numerous mammalian species, and just the act of living—every one of us has to breathe the air, we have to drink water, eat food, clothe and shelter ourselves.	
And it doesn't end there. Ever since the end of World War II, we've been afflicted with an incredible appetite for stuff.	
We go to a store to buy a cotton shirt; I'm sure there are very few of you that ask, "Gee, is this cotton shirt organic?"	
And yet, the very act of buying these products has repercussions that extend around the world.	
Scientists divide the history of Earth into the different epochs—periods of geological time.	*Eocene, Holocene, Miocene and Pleistocene … Paul Crutzen says that this period should be called the Anthropocene epoch:*
We've got to come to grips with the immensity of our power and our impact on the planet.	
A few years ago, I went to a, a village high up in the mountains of the Andes in Peru.	

After You Listen

Suzuki says that we see the world through personal experiences. How do your experiences shape your attitudes toward the environment? How might these attitudes differ from a person living in the developing world? Discuss your answers in a group.

_____

_____

_____

_____

WARM-UP ASSIGNMENT
Introduce a Speaker

If you have not done so already, sooner or later you will be asked to introduce a speaker in an academic or work setting. An introduction involves saying something about the person's background and expertise, as well as the presentation topic and the reasons the audience should be interested. In this assignment, you will choose a speaker and introduce him or her.

A. Read the following introduction of David Suzuki.

> David Suzuki is an award-winning scientist, environmentalist and broadcaster. He is co-founder of the David Suzuki Foundation, which works with government, business and individuals to conserve our environment by providing science-based research, education and policy. He is renowned for his radio and television programs that explain the complexities of the natural sciences in a compelling, easily understood way.

> Although he is a third-generation Canadian, as a child he was interned with his family and other Japanese Canadians during World War II. After settling in Ontario, Canada, he excelled in school and, at university, studied biology and zoology. He held posts at different universities in the US before accepting a position at the University of British Columbia, where he conducted research in genetics and where he is now Professor Emeritus.

B. Based on these biographical notes, what might you expect Suzuki to talk about? Choose one example and write a one- or two-sentence introduction to a presentation topic.

Tonight, David Suzuki will be speaking about _____

_____

_____

_____

_____

C. Look for a short speech, or part of a longer speech, by a well-known environmentalist. You may find an important historical speech in the library or a more recent one on the Internet. Choose a speech that will be interesting for other students. Speak with your teacher and ask for approval of your choice.

D. Research the speaker. Keep a record of your sources. Which elements of the speaker's background and expertise relate to the speech you have chosen? Any speaker might have a great many biographical details, but only a few of these details would be both important to the topic and relevant to establishing the speaker as an expert. For someone who has had a long and distinguished career, note only the highlights.

_____

_____

_____

_____

_____

E. The topic and tone of a speech are important and are often determined by each audience. Good speakers adjust the topic for different audiences. For example, the director of a green technologies company could speak about the future of the technology industry, first to a board of directors and then to a high-school class, but the speeches would be different. Part of the difference could be in the content, but the tone of the speeches (e.g., humorous, cautionary, motivational, informational) might also differ. Review your chosen speech and answer the following questions.

① What is the general topic? _____

② Who is the audience? _____

③ What is the tone of the speech? _____

F. When you have a good understanding of both the speaker and the speech, consider what reason or reasons the audience might have for listening. Reasons might include an interest in learning something new, a desire to be entertained or a need for information that will help them make a decision.

_____

_____

_____

_____

_____

G. Put your ideas together and prepare a brief introduction that does not borrow content from the presentation but gives the audience an idea of who the speaker is, as well as good reasons for listening to the speech. In a group, take turns presenting your introductions.

_____

_____

_____

_____

_____

_____

_____

Signposting

When you read a page, there are many clues about where you are in the text, what's coming next and how long the passage will continue. Moreover, if the information is difficult to understand, you can read more slowly and go back a step to clarify a point. Picking up on these types of clues is more difficult when listening to a presentation, so good speakers help an audience by signposting their speeches. Signposting helps guide listeners from one idea to another.

Asking rhetorical questions helps focus listeners' attention. You don't expect listeners to answer aloud.

A. Read the following signposting functions and consider how they are used. Which ones do you commonly use when you give a presentation? For each function, add one more example of a typical phrase used in signposting a speech.

SIGNPOSTING FUNCTION	EXAMPLE PHRASES	YOUR PHRASE
BEGINNING A NEW TOPIC	I would like to start by … Let's begin by looking at …	
LISTING	First, I'd like to explain … Second, …	
FINISHING A TOPIC AND MOVING ON	So that covers … Now, let's talk about … Now that we've explored …, we can …	
EXPANDING ON AN IDEA	To explain what I mean, … To give you a better idea, …	
REFORMULATING AN IDEA	Another way of saying that is … By this I mean …	
GIVING AN EXAMPLE	For example, … To give you an example, …	
GIVING A REASON	This is … because … The reason for this is …	
SHOWING SIMILARITY	This is the same as … There's no difference between … and …	
SHOWING CONTRAST	However, this is … This is different from …	
ASKING A RHETORICAL QUESTION	So, what does this mean? The question is, …?	
CONCLUDING	In conclusion, … In summary, …	

B. Read the following sentences from the chapter listenings and identify the signposting function of each.

SENTENCE	SIGNPOSTING FUNCTION
❶ First of all, slow down.	_____
❷ So what then at this moment is the challenge?	_____
❸ Al Gore, for example, has famously described climate change as a moral issue.	_____
❹ Of course, the reason we were so undistinguished was that our secret was hidden.	_____
❺ Consider our numbers: 10,000 years ago, ... it's estimated there were ten million human beings on the entire planet.	_____
❻ In other words, the smaller you are, the more of you there can be.	_____

C. Work with a partner and practise reading the sentences in task B aloud. Then, practise saying them in your own words, substituting other signposting phrases for the ones used.

FOCUS ON LISTENING

Listening for Audience Questions

After a presentation, a speaker will often invite the audience to ask questions. One of the challenges in answering such questions is in understanding exactly what is being asked. Sometimes a question may be buried in other rambling information, such as the audience member expressing thanks and giving background to the question. Other times, there may be several questions together or even no questions at all.

A. Read the excerpt from Listening 3 and the explanatory notes. With a partner, discuss what makes the question at the end easy or difficult to understand.

This audience member introduces himself and thanks the speaker. →

"Hello, my name is Anton, and I'd like to thank you, Mr. Suzuki, for coming and visiting us in Perth. I'm not sure so much if this is a question, but it is in its own right.

← *It seems he has not clarified the question in his own mind.*

He gives background in the form of biography. →

"Every day, well not every day, but on some given days, I travel home from work, and I contemplate what role it is that I play as part of humanity, and trying to get out of the rat race. You know, I'm an ambitious person; I'm trying to build a business. I'm trying to put myself in a position where I'm going to be able to support a family.

← *He's trying to say he's conflicted about building a business and working to support a family versus pursuing his desire for a non-traditional job.*

It's difficult to know how a question will relate to this background information. →

He shifts from talking about himself to people in general. ———→

> "But at that same time I'm thinking: what is it that I am doing, or what is it that I'm not doing, that's gonna sustain our ability to be able to live long into the future?

*The last "can" in the question appears to be about sustaining life (i.e., what can **we** do so ——→ that **we** can "… live long into the future"), but it's not clear.*

> "And I suppose the question that I ask is: what can I do right now to change so I can?"

←——— *It's difficult to relate his point about living long into the future to his question.*

B. Working on your own, summarize the excerpt in task A into one or two clear questions.

_____

_____

_____

_____

C. Here is another question from a different audience member, also from Listening 3. A lot of what he says is unnecessary. Identify the essential information and reduce the excerpt to one or two more direct questions.

> "Hello? Hello, David, my name is Demush and I really love you. And, [laughter] and thank you, thank you … I love your ideas, and I love what you said, and I've been living in Perth for ten years. And I would like to know why you're actually coming to Perth. Because with all what you said—this is, Josh presented you before, and well, presented Perth, saying it is the most unsustainable city in Australia. We have so many things going wrong here. Why are you actually coming here?"

_____

_____

_____

_____

D. Share your questions from tasks B and C with a partner. How do your versions compare?

E. Listen to Suzuki's responses to the two audience questions, in Listening 3.

LISTENING 3

The Legacy: An Elder's Vision for Our Sustainable Future, Part 2

In the second part of Suzuki's speech, he tries to inspire his audience by asking them to imagine an alternative world in which we leave a smaller ecological footprint and live in better balance with the environment and with other species.

Before You Listen

In the Focus on Speaking (page 159), you learned how speakers use signposting to help guide listeners. Read the excerpt on the next page and identify which techniques Suzuki uses.

"... And I think of Aboriginal people around the world who see the Earth as sacred because she is our mother, for whom rocks and rivers and forests and soil are sacred. How do you put a value on something that is sacred? And that's the problem when we evaluate everything in economic terms; those things that matter most to us have no value at all in our economic system. Somehow, we've got ourselves into thinking that we need more and more, bigger and better, more recent, more modern—and that's going to make us happy. And yet, we know in our hearts that's not true."

_____

_____

_____

While You Listen

In a large portion of this segment of Suzuki's speech, he uses repetition to give a vision for the future, starting thirteen sentences with the word *imagine*. The first time you listen, try to get the general idea. Listen a second time and take notes on each segment: the world Suzuki is encouraging you to imagine and his answers to questions from the audience. Listen a third time to check your notes and add details.

SEGMENT	NOTES
... re-imagine the future ...	
Imagine a world where we live, work and play in the same area.	
Imagine where the streets and, and houses and roads all have the ability to trap every bit of sunlight falling on it ...	
Imagine every roof ...	
Imagine our cities filled with orchards of fruit and nut trees, and community gardens ...	
Imagine extracting heat from the Earth in the winter ...	
Imagine cancer and asthma rates plummeting ...	
Imagine zero production of waste ...	

SEGMENT	NOTES
Imagine, as I was, as I did when I was a kid, ...	
Imagine catching a fish and eating it without worrying about what's in it.	
Imagine an Australia with rich forests that can be logged forever ...	
Imagine lighter-than-air ships that transport massive payloads ...	
Imagine taking tourists on wonderful trips across the Earth ...	
Imagine an economy that is in balance with nature's productive capacity, ...	
So let us dream of what is possible ...	
RESPONSE TO AUDIENCE QUESTION 1	
... one of the most important legacies I leave is my foundation.	*Goal: to identify people anxious to make a change, then train them to begin the discussion, offer tools and resources* *Slogan: We want to motivate the motivated to motivate.* *Website: davidsuzuki.org*
... we're just a drop in the bucket— ...	
RESPONSE TO AUDIENCE QUESTION 2	
... you have to look at your own, your own life and lifestyle and the way you consume.	
We need at this time—you know, there are all kinds of suggestions about what you can do on our website.	*The Nature Challenge:* *Useful, simple, effective if enough of us do them*
So we've got to slow down, but we've got to also get off the path.	

After You Listen

Reflect on Suzuki's vision for a more environmentally friendly future. Which suggestions would be easy for you and your community to adopt? Which would be difficult? Why? Discuss your answers in a group.

Academic
Survival Skill

Learning Discussion Techniques for Examining Problems

In lengthy lectures and presentations, audience members are often reluctant to ask questions. Instead, they wait, hoping someone else will ask. One way to encourage more participation is to use alternative discussion formats that inspire audience members to consider and solve problems.

A. Review the following four ways to get audience members to interact beyond simply asking individual questions. Work in small groups to discuss the pros and cons of each, and write down your ideas.

TECHNIQUE	PROS	CONS
AUDIENCE REACTION TEAM: Before the presentation, a small group of audience members are given the task of summarizing and interpreting the presentation and also of asking questions.		
BUZZ GROUP: The group is divided into smaller groups, each of which is given a single topic or different questions to discuss and report back on to the group.		
FISHBOWL: A part of the larger group forms a circle in the centre of the room and discusses and debates the topic while the larger group listens and asks questions.		
THINK, PAIR, SHARE: One or more questions are presented to the group, and students think about them, find a partner and discuss their ideas. They then share their conclusions as a group.		

B. Consider this quotation from Indian revolutionary Mahatma Gandhi (1869–1948).

"Earth provides enough to satisfy every man's needs, but not every man's greed."

Assuming this to be true, then what is the solution to the issue of sustainability addressed in David Suzuki's lecture? Work with a partner and use the think, pair, share technique to discuss answers to this question. Take notes, and then present your ideas to the class. This will help you prepare for the Final Assignment, in which you will use the same technique to come up with questions for speakers at a town hall meeting.

_____

_____

_____

_____

_____

_____

_____

FINAL ASSIGNMENT
Take Part in a Town Hall Meeting

Now it's your turn. Use everything you have learned in this chapter to prepare for and participate in a town hall-style meeting.

A. As a class, decide on an environmental issue currently being debated in the news. This will be the topic of the town hall meeting. Topics might include issues related to alternative energy sources, resource management, habitat loss for one or more species, nuclear energy or the transportation of oil and gas.

TOPIC: _____

B. The teacher will assign one member of the class the role of moderator. The moderator will prepare and present a brief introduction to the topic and, after the presentations from the speakers, will lead the question period. The rest of the class will form groups of four to six students. In your group, choose one of the environmentalists identified in the Warm-Up Assignment (page 157). Share your choice with the moderator, who will write up and post a program of speakers.

C. One member of your group will act as speaker in the town hall discussion, playing the role of the environmentalist. Another member will introduce the speaker, although this is normally the job of the moderator. Your teacher will randomly assign the speaker and introducer roles just before the meeting, so everyone in your group must be prepared to assume either role.

D. Research the topic and prepare for the presentation as a group. Find out more about your environmentalist and his or her point of view, expanding on the information gathered for the Warm-Up Assignment. Keep complete records of each source. Write an introduction that emphasizes the speaker's connection to the topic. Imagine what he or she might say, or look for quotations and use them as starting points.

E. Using the think, pair, share technique, prepare with your group to participate as active audience members supporting your speaker with critical insights and practical suggestions. From the program posted by the moderator, consider other groups' speakers and research their backgrounds, too; you will need to prepare questions for their presentations.

F. Plan your presentation. The point of a town hall meeting is to share ideas in a larger group. Use the following table to organize your notes.

PRESENTATION STRUCTURE	NOTES
The moderator briefly introduces the topic.	
Each speaker is introduced by a member of his or her group.	

PRESENTATION STRUCTURE	NOTES
After the introductions, speakers take five to ten minutes to outline their points of view on the topic, offering both criticisms and suggestions.	
As each speaker addresses the topic, everyone takes notes and considers questions.	
Once the speakers have presented their ideas, the moderator invites audience groups to think, pair and share. Group members then try to think of the best questions for the speakers as well as general comments that can help fuel the conversation with both the speakers and the other members of the audience.	
The moderator opens the town hall meeting to questions from the floor. The moderator may let group members pose questions to a particular speaker directly or may decide a question is suitable for all the speakers to answer.	
After all the questions have been asked, the moderator allows each speaker two minutes to offer concluding remarks.	

G. As separate groups, practise taking part in a town hall meeting, using the structure given.

H. In the town hall meeting, take an active part: challenge the speakers with probing questions.

"Never doubt that a small group of thoughtful, committed citizens can change the world. Indeed, it's the only thing that ever has."
—Margaret Mead, American anthropologist (1901–1978)

CRITICAL CONNECTIONS

Chapters 7 and 8 both dealt with research and learning from the dead and the dying: in Chapter 7, we looked at learning from cadavers, and in Chapter 8, from extinct or endangered species. Now you have the opportunity to put together everything you've learned and think critically to complete integrated tasks.

Sohn (2011) writes about the death of the Neanderthals, early hominids that coexisted with our ancestors. She reports on controversial studies that have concluded that climate change—in this case, the arrival of an ice age—was partly responsible for the disappearance of the Neanderthals. Read the following excerpt, in which she explains that travelling farther for food resulted in inter-breeding between Neanderthals and early humans.

> "New research says Neanderthals didn't go extinct, but instead their genes were essentially swallowed up into the human genome. When climate took a turn toward the cold, tens of thousands of years ago, both Nean-derthals and early humans started travelling further distances to find food" (Sohn, 2011).

1. With a partner, use the think, pair, share technique (see the Academic Survival Skill on page 164) to discuss the excerpt and consider other ways in which the changing climate might have contributed to the disappearance of the Nean-derthals. Share ideas in a group.

2. Climate change affects many animal species by changing their habitats, often destroying their sources of food and shelter. How would some of the factors you identified in the disappearance of the Neanderthals be similar among animal species? Discuss your ideas in a group.

3. In some countries hit hard by climate change, humans, too, are being forced to leave their homes because of flooding, drought and rising temperatures. Culturally, what consequences might forced migration have on these peoples? Discuss your ideas in a group.

Reference

Sohn, E. (2011). Climate change may have doomed Neanderthals. *Discovery News*. Retrieved from http://news.discovery.com/history/neanderthals-adapt-climate-change-111118.html

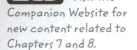
Visit the Companion Website for new content related to Chapters 7 and 8.

PHOTO CREDITS

ALAMY

pp. viii, 22–23, 42, 43 © Danita Delimont; p. 154 bottom © fotoviva.

CORBIS

Cover, p. iii © Tim Pannell/Corbis.

ISTOCKPHOTO

p. 150 top © EdStock.

SHUTTERSTOCK

pp. viii, 64–65, 81, 83 © kwest; pp. vii, ix, 84–85, 103, 125 © 1000 Words; pp. ix, 104–105, 123, 125 © Kiselev Andrey Valerevich; pp. ix, 126–127, 144, 167 © Allison Achauer; pp. ix, 146–147, 165, 167 © sochigirl; p. 3 © Maisei Raman; p. 5 © Mikael Damkier; p. 6 © dotshock; p. 7 © Yuri Arcurs; p. 23 top left © zebrik; p. 23 bottom left © africa924; p. 23 top right © fritz16; p. 23 bottom right © Northfoto; p. 26 © Darrin Henry; p. 27 © ErickN; p. 32 © Daniel Prudek; p. 33 left © Hung Chung Chih; p. 33 right © Monkey Business Images; p. 35 © great_photos; p. 37 © Sadequl Hussain; p. 38 © euko; p. 40 © JGW Images; p. 41 © Boris Stroujko; p. 50 © Miro Kovacevic; p. 59 © mezzotint; p. 69 top © chere; p. 69 bottom © Dmitrijs Bindemanis; p. 73 © dutourdumonde; p. 74 © Bikeworldtravel; p. 76 © Tomas Urbelionis Photo; p. 87 top © arindambanerjee; p. 87 bottom © Brendan Howard; p. 109 left © CLIPAREA; p. 109 right © YAKOBCHUK VASYL; p. 116 © CreativeNature.nl; p. 117 © Pact-Shot; p. 136 © Reeed; p. 150 bottom left © Marco Uliana; p. 150 bottom middle © Eric Isselee; p. 150 bottom right © a9photo.

THINKSTOCK

pp. viii, 2–3, 20, 43; pp. viii, 44–45, 62, 83; p. 8; p. 9; p. 11; p. 12; p. 13; p. 14; p. 15; p. 16; p. 25; p. 30; p. 31; p. 39; p. 45; p. 47; p. 48; p. 49; p. 53; p. 56; p. 57; p. 61; p. 67; p. 70; p. 78; p. 80; p. 89; p. 90; p. 91; p. 93; p. 94; p. 96; p. 98; p. 100; p. 107; p. 108; p. 109 top; p. 110; p. 112; p. 113 top; p. 114; p. 116; p. 119; p. 121; p. 122; p. 129; p. 130; p. 131; p. 133; p. 134; p. 135; p. 137; p. 139; p. 140; p. 142; p. 143; p. 144; p. 149; p. 150 middle left; p. 152; p. 154 top; p. 155; p. 157; p. 158; p. 160; p. 162.